BERLIN W,
OR, MÉSALLIANCE

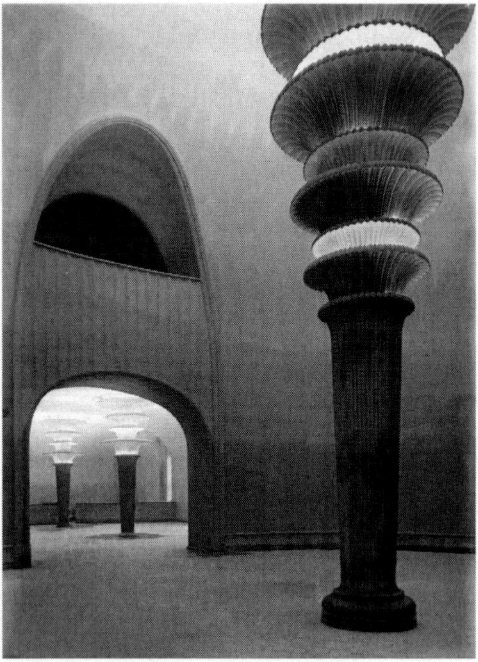

SIMON WORTHAM

BERLIN W,
OR, MÉSALLIANCE
POSTHUMOUS FRAGMENTS
PETER MÜLLER

THE CONSTELLATIONS, BOOK XXVI

MA BIBLIOTHÈQUE, LONDON
 Published 2022
Printed by Printed World Publishing, Hastings, Great Britain
Set in Didot & Bodoni Ornaments

ISBN 978-1-910055-94-6

Papers used are from well-managed forests and responsible sources

Image credit, page 107:
Reg Butler, 1951–52, Third Maquette for 'The Unknown Political Prisoner',
© The Estate of Reg Butler. Photo: Tate

SIMON WORTHAM

BERLIN W, OR, MÉSALLIANCE

POSTHUMOUS FRAGMENTS

PETER MÜLLER

MA BIBLIOTHÈQUE

Since arriving in Berlin, I've lost the habit of finding humanity laughable.

— Robert Walser

EDITOR'S NOTE

THESE ARE THE LAST of the papers of any substance to be released by the estate of Peter Müller. Shortly before his death, Peter's brother Luca replied to a speculative request on my part, to which I had received no response for several months, with a hundred or so handwritten pages (the handwriting just as tiny as ever, at the very limits of legibility in fact, and always at risk of crossing the border into the margins). I had almost forgotten that I asked, and was incredibly surprised by the package that arrived, without any explanation, in a plain padded envelope on a cold, bright morning in October, my garden wet with fallen leaves and, beneath the trees, the forgotten clues of a dead summer. I recall that the postage had not been adequately covered, and it is one of the many things that makes me laugh when I think about this particular editorial experience, just as Peter's writing often makes me laugh as one sometimes does in the middle of the night after waking from strange dreams. The papers included what appeared to be a preliminary sketch for an academic publication, marked 'Notes on the Typology of a Neurosis'. It is important to recognise, however, that Müller never published anything substantial on psychoanalysis; the writings that appeared during his lifetime make scant reference to Freud or any of his followers or detractors. In with these notes was another set of pages describing Müller's time in West Berlin during the 1970s. It is a memoir, of sorts. At its centre is a woman with, perhaps, another name than her own. But there is also other material about Berlin itself, which might best be described as 'assorted'. The story of Berlin, and the story of Müller's experience of the city, is told through a variety of literary, historical, and architectural vignettes that become entangled with his reflections upon a love affair—an affair that seems to carry a political charge as much as an existential one. These are without doubt the most explicitly personal writings by Müller I have encountered, even though all his work seems to tremble with feeling—whether about childhood, art, war, or memory—and even though these particular texts are not devoid of the enigmatic reserve, the slightly formal and sometimes antiquated style, that characterises almost every page he wrote. In many respects, the tale is told rather quickly, summarily, one might say. But at times the prose thickens into a poetry, the cameos of Berlin are as disconcerting they are striking—arresting would be a good word—and the overall impression is of a heavy object moving at high speed, like a bomb. Breathlessness is a motif that repeats itself throughout, often in a horrifying sense. The psychoanalytic notes seem to invite biographical interpretation and, although one should be extremely cautious, it is as if they possess a degree of explanatory power in relation to the events that unfold in Berlin. At any rate, the depiction of human experience—psychic experience—under particular conditions does seem to cross borders, back and forth, between one and the other. Given that the writing on Freud dwells at considerable length on the effects of a false connection, we should be wary—although, of course, the Berlin story is nothing if not a case of the very same thing. The problem is that every clue might be a false or even falsely false trace of something else (in other words, evidence designed to mislead us it is not true).

I was unable to ask Luca Müller why all these pages had become mixed up, for they did not arrive as separate texts but were shuffled together haphazardly, it seems, although I have not changed their order for publication. It is impossible to say whether Peter meant them to be read in this way—

if, as is no doubt questionable, he meant them to be read at all. Or whether they were, in any sense, complete (as is the case with all of his posthumous work). Neither is it possible to date them precisely or, for that matter, to know if they derive from exactly the same period in time. I hesitated over these last writings, having serious misgivings whether I should bring them into the public domain. That they form a sort of autobiographical pair (or more than a pair—for there are at least three, not only two, names on the roll call) is, as I have said, justifiably a matter of debate; but what swayed me is not only that the texts had somehow been preserved, deliberately or not, but that they were composed in a way that obviously relied on the sense of a reader. Of course, these pages will not reach the widest of audiences: the writing is not only difficult and perhaps rather self-involved in places, but it is dated in the sense that it covers topics and explores ways of thinking that are considered by many to be almost obsolete. To risk extending the analogy, perhaps the papers I pulled out of that bubble-lined envelope in the low sunshine of an autumn morning are destined to remain an unexploded bomb. Nevertheless, I felt, without being able to back up the feeling, that they were meant to be read.

The title under which these pieces are published is entirely mine, although hopefully the following pages justify the choice. I realise I have not mentioned that I was also unable to question Luca about the identity of the woman in Berlin. I am afraid to say that his death precluded such a conversation, although I have no way of knowing if he would have responded, or even if he knew anything about it. I suspect we may never know which, if either, was her real identity—if she ever existed at all.

S.K.

LIESL

LIESL REISSMANN, SO SHE TOLD ME, was born in Wittenberg in Spring 1948, in a quiet suburb untroubled by the Allied bombs that struck the nearby Arado Flugzeugwerke towards the end of the war, killing the slave-labourers from Poland and Russia, mostly young Jewish women, in their hundreds. Liesl had worked in domestic service from late childhood, she told me, because her parents, having become estranged, both died at a young age. In her early twenties she managed to cross the border, living in Freiberg for a time, working as a hairdresser apparently, before travelling to Switzerland, first Zürich then Bern, serving as a hospital orderly and suffering an unwanted pregnancy in circumstances that I never quite understood but which brought her to Berlin, childless and alone. She was tall and pale, with freckled skin and blonde eyelashes, her hair the colour of damp straw, and I remember that while she seldom smoked cigarettes there was always a soft pack of Filter Kings in the shoulder bag she carried, half-buried beneath unopened letters, coupons, various forms of identification, a driving license, passport, crumpled receipts, blank postcards, and packets of pocket tissues. She never wore make-up, though it was in the bag too. And old keys and broken pens and, I supposed, some family pictures in a little leather wallet. Her coat was always longer than her skirt and she was always late, although never so late that anybody would lose patience or leave before she arrived.

Liesl was almost thirty when I knew her and living in a small place in Kreuzberg that she rented from a Turkish family one storey below. I had rooms in Zehlendorf, to the south-west near the botanical gardens, because I was teaching at the Free University. What brought us together was books, I suppose. She had joined a seminar taught in the classroom next to mine; on a canteen break I found her reading *The Gulag Archipelago*, in the French edition, which hadn't been out more than a couple of years, and we argued about it over coffee. Liesl started sitting in on my lectures. I can't remember much about the time before I met her in Berlin, or about the time it took us to know each other. We just suddenly did, as if we always had. We were so unalike. She was confident, expansive—conspicuous, I'm tempted to say—in a way that, although I never thought about it, suited her background rather badly. Her conversation was sometimes broken, but eloquent and often compelling; with a book open, Liesl's absorption was just as expressive, and just as curious. She read with one eye shut, or half-shut, her head tilted to one side, her hands clasped tight around the pages like she was at the wheel of a speeding car. Almost as if she was taking aim.

As for myself, after I had taught my classes I often spent the afternoon walking among the light shadows of the Viktoriahaus, through gardens of blue-green foliage with their velvet lawns and American trees, or I'd walk up through the streets that led past the Brücke Museum to the forest. At night-time, if I wasn't working, I would sometimes go up to one of the bars we knew at the edge of the city if I knew Liesl would be there, but more often I would work. At that time, I was writing something on Friedrich Dürrenmatt, and it wasn't going well. I had the politics of it too much at the front of my mind—not just Dürrenmatt, but the whole of post-war drama—as though a concrete bypass had been thrown up over a dwindling landscape. So I'd end up telephoning Liesl, and we'd drink a beer or some brandies in the cellar of some old building or other, sitting on broken stools, talking about this and that—something she'd read or a restaurant she'd been to, the ghost stations of the U-Bahn, the American wars, what I was writing. I kept off the underground as far as possible. The division of Berlin meant there were trains passing through tunnels that crossed from West to East and back again, there were platforms at which one never stopped, and some lines one just avoided for the sake of convenience as much as anything. Most of the war-damage had been rectified years ago, and the network had in fact been extended along its north-south axis, with new sections opened in haste after the autumn of 1961. But because of the history of the last half-century, some tunnels went nowhere, some platforms were planned though never appeared, routine circumnavigations took place of which one was sometimes only dimly aware (although sometimes keenly so), and it was as if parts of the U-Bahn existed as an X-ray of a smashed body put back together through a spate of battlefield operations rushed along in a makeshift theatre. Badly set breaks to the bone caused the limbs to behave strangely in pursuing their function, the result of a misalignment or a 'malunion' as the doctors would say. All in all, it was as if a clandestine anatomy existed just beneath the cartographical skin of the city, a metropolitan unconscious whose repression was administered with the grimly intricate diligence of a train timetable.

My way to Liesl was an overground route that transected West Berlin across an ascending diagonal, up through the old Prussian districts of Steglitz and past the municipal parks of Schöneberg into the heart of things. Gone were the electric trams upon which Robert Walser rode during his Berlin years, composing delicate melodies to the rhythm of their movement, the streets outside glazed and grey in the rain, rumbling on past squares and bridges, a ministry building or a department store. I had not been in love before, so didn't know that I was, not until afterwards. I don't know what she knew about it – how I felt, I mean. She came to me the night after we had laughed together about Solzhenitsyn. It was that quick. She came to the door with a bottle of vermouth, interrupting a paragraph I was stuck on, lost in *Der Blinde* and the Thirty Years' War, slumped among the ruins of castle in an empty land, as blind as Dürrenmatt's duke himself. Afterwards we talked about Bern, where the typescript of the play was archived, and where through certain medical connections she had arranged a termination less than a year earlier. She was lovely, I thought, just so lovely, and having thought it I never needed to think it again.

In a 'malunion' of broken bone, an outgrowth forms at the shattered limits of the break, the lack of a true connection creating twisted, calcified matter. Liesl's name, of German and Hebrew origin, apparently means 'God is my oath'. She told me that, I remember, during a visit to the Neue Nationalgalerie, the last of Mies van der Rohe's skin-and-bones, a stone stronghold of modernism with a glass box for a lookout station. We gazed at the paintings while she told me about her childhood. She could have talked, as I thought she might, about the pioneers and the Free German Youth, Wittenberg in the fifties, holidays on the Baltic coast, or the television; instead, she told me about a boy she loved when she was thirteen, younger than her, and how they had gone into some trees and made a fire and left it behind thinking it was dead but later on, making their way back along the path, it had flared up and they were cut off, and she had run past the flames and left him behind. Two days later, when she saw him on the street, Liesl remembered she had not told anyone about it, and he passed her by, careful not to look up, and they never spoke again. We would sometimes go to galleries on a Sunday or a Saturday, rarely to discuss the pictures at any length, but instead to make small talk or trade university rumour as we drifted from room to room. Occasionally I would offer some remarks about this or that painting, but more often she would just tilt her head and make a small sound, indicating disapproval or acquiescing to a particular piece, before swivelling on her heels as if to rotate the conversation back to the classrooms and corridors of FU. The underground bunker of the Neue Nationalgalerie was a roll call in cubism and abstraction. Werner Haftmann—a grey-looking fellow and erstwhile Italianist—had been the director until recently, establishing the collection in the late sixties through an opportunistic combination of loans, gifts, and acquisitions bent on restoring the decimated ruins of the avant-garde. A founder of Documenta with Arnold Bode a decade earlier, Haftmann's schtick was to parade the modern art once labelled degenerate as a force for progressive internationalism after the war. He was mercurial—there was talk about him, going as far back as the thirties. Ill-health had seen him replaced, and now it was Dieter Honisch, a Silesian and fellow Pole, who ran the show. Liesl seemed distant, her mind on other things. The gallery obviously left her cold. We stood outside, the rain having eased, and it was as if we had both just woken up, even though we were rarely awkward in each other's company. The rain started again, and we ran through the streets for longer than we would have liked, ducking into a café for some cover. And suddenly Liesl was alive once more, and all the colours came back, and we were closed in a dream that was warm and full of life, the sound of forks and knives and the smell of soup and dumplings and warm bread. You are funny, she said, the way you like to collect pictures and words, and put them in an order, and look and them and have others look at them, but really, they are only for you and you do it in a way that nobody else really sees. And you build room after room of exhibits, books, and paintings, and bits of history and memory, and you expect me to look but not to touch, or not to look even. But I love you for it, somehow, I love you even so. I don't blame you, I'm rather like you in fact. And she reached across the table for my hand, her eyes smiling. I'm just the sorting-table, aren't I? I'm a psychic writing-pad, she said, and you mark out the letters and the words thinking they're yours, but knowing they're not, and never knowing the traces that survive when you want to start again. Scratched out on the wax of me. All the small imperfections you leave behind without knowing it, I'm yours in that sense more than any other. I couldn't tell how far she was being playful. Her eyes shone and her hands tightened around mine. It was only later that evening I realised what she had said, that she loved me. She hadn't said it before. Alone, in the darkness, before falling asleep, I could not get comfortable and in the end, I read until it was very late.

That night I dreamt of Ernst Kirchner's street scene of the Potsdamer Platz, painted just before the outbreak of hostilities in 1914. On awakening, it made me think of a picture Robert Walser's brother had made eleven years earlier, called *The Dream*. I guess that was why, because they were very different pieces. I'd been writing about Walser, to get a break from the post-war theatre: Karl Walser had illustrated his brother's first book, *Fritz Kocher's Essays*, published in 1904 by Insel Verlag with eleven drawings, which hardly sold and for which neither were ever paid. I don't know from where the Kirchner came. In 1914, the coming war had changed the palette from Karl's dreamy pinks and azure blues to bile green and angry salmon. The floating curves of a turn-of-the-century stage designer had mutated, a decade later, into the sharp angles of a saloon table tipped over in a fight. The midnight figures in the Kirchner—nothing like Karl Walser's pierrot strolling in the empty air with his surreal, chiffon-caked paramour—nevertheless recalled the odd couple in *The Dream* because they were as connected and separate as the two bodies in a lunar eclipse. The tight dresses of each woman were fringed at an oblique angle above high heels, their slanted faces topped by feathered hats, dead black sockets sunk deep above precipitous avocado cheekbones. The painting seemed as garishly lit as their scarlet lips, the yellow quills like a cheap firework display. Walser's drifted into vision, lingering like a memory that never was. Kirchner's was a dying world screaming at the future. I remembered Liesl, and the boy in the fire.

NOTES ON THE TYPOLOGY OF A NEUROSIS

NOTE 1: Early in the course of his treatment of obsessional neurosis in a young man of university education, racked with guilt after his father's death, Freud treats his patient to a sly preview of the underlying essentials of psychoanalysis. The study took place in Vienna between 1907 and 1908, around the same time that Robert Walser was writing his stories of Berlin, of the old Asinger, of the street markets selling sprats and liverwurst, the Tiergarten and Friedrichstrasse, the indolent commotion and kaleidoscopic cartography of a town with no prescience of its future. The illness is so debilitating for the subject in question that solace is sought by him in the encouraging words of a friend, who insists that the young man's continual self-reproach is disproportionate and unwarranted. Freud summarily dismisses this crumb of comfort, while at the same time taking it as the opportunity to reflect on the psychic circumstance of a 'false connection'. Those who downplay certain psychological reactions on the grounds that they are not justified by the facts are guilty of missing the point, says Freud. The affect is never too great for the occasion, it has just been misattributed. The content is not absent, it is just elsewhere. To pursue a false connection runs the risk of those police forces who, when they cannot catch the right murderer, readily apprehend the wrong one instead. Nevertheless, the mistake made by the friend of Freud's obsessive case – later known, famously, as the Rat Man – is to assume there has been no murder, which is out of the question.

Freud has a particular word for this mismatch between the affect and its content, between the intensity of the psychic reaction and the occasion for it. He calls it a *mésalliance*.

A bad marriage. In the space of a few sentences, obsessional neurosis calls up the family drama as both an ill-fated romance and a crime scene. Psychoanalysis 101. But the connection between the two is curious. It is as if, from an analytic point of view, there is only a crime scene – a 'whodunnit?' – because of the false connection or bad match. And if it is true, if the son is guilty of violating his father, if there is always a murder, then surely by the same token every marriage is in peril of becoming a *mésalliance*. Every connection, in other words, risks becoming the cause of a fatal wrongdoing made all the more terrible, all the more inevitable, by the fact that it might never really have happened. This leaves psychoanalysis, like a rogue cop in the movies, hanging on to its job but with its work cut out. And, as Freud himself observes, the situation is made worse by the fact that evidence deteriorates from the moment it is dug up, as the example of Pompeii's excavation makes abundantly clear. The long-preserved features of the unconscious persist so long as they remain untouched, packed in ashes as it were; analysis risks corrupting its findings in the course of their exposure. The terrible denial made possible at Nuremberg was premised on the idea that actual evidence of the wrong disintegrated in the gas chambers, that whomsoever survived could not by definition testify to the absolute destruction that was being claimed. Perhaps the predicament of psychoanalysis is not like that; perhaps its vocation is in total conflict with such thinking. What's missing, what are we missing? – that's always the question, and it never stops, never lets itself falter through lack of evidence, which is always a kind of evidence. But, still, it always risks a *mésalliance*, a bad scene.

In order to characterise it better, Freud draws a distinction between obsessional neurosis and hysteria, on which his earlier studies concentrated at length. Whereas the hysteric confronts the psychic tensions by which they are afflicted through acts of compromise, inflicting upon themselves a simultaneous combination of affects—seeking impossibly to kill two elusive birds with one jagged stone—compulsive behaviour separates into distinct and consecutive parts. In the conflict between primary motives and the subsequent psychological reaction to them, second-stage actions do not negotiate their own causes so much as they compulsively rationalise them in a way that is tantamount to denial. The displacement of the original material is conducted according to a certain logic on which it rather madly depends, giving rise to intractable routines, ornate rituals, laboriously intricate plans, impossibly pristine scruples. The obsessional neurotic therefore finds themselves powerless in the face of compulsive demands that—however lucid and meticulous—repeatedly miss the mark, as it were, purposely failing to appreciate their own precipitating impulses. Hence obsessions are mostly pursued self-reproachfully. (Such reproach—the hallmark of the obsessive—easily turns into brooding self-doubt, shame, and then, often, hypochondriacal anxiety, social anxiety, moral or religious anxiety, delusions of conspicuousness to others, fear of lapses of conscience, a continual testing of self, precautionary or penitential measures designed to alleviate the condition they express, and so on; sometimes even a shallow sense of superiority derived from obsessive conscientiousness. In the end, the sufferer may resort to drinking as readily as hoarding or prayer in response to their own illness.) But having connected their affects with the wrong causes, compulsives can quite coldly dismiss facets of the original malady when they do arise. They may be much less bothered by a wayward and telling sexual allusion than a miskept timetable; they might obsess over a poorly folded hand towel next to a filthy toilet.

While compulsive behaviour is highly structured, its elements can be peculiarly heterogeneous—understandably so, given the nature of its defence against repressed material that can itself be extremely complex and contradictory. Obsessional logic is often as strained as it is punctilious. For this reason, perhaps, Freud is minded to speak of obsessive thinking rather than simply habitual actions. That is the thing to really understand. In the case of obsession, as he puts it, the armaments of reason are co-opted in the interests of pathological thought (as if it were ever possible to psychically decommission reason's weaponry). Freud names such structures of thinking deliria. Compulsive thinking on the part of the neurotic avails itself of a grammar—a wording of their own ideas, Freud says—which his patients themselves cannot readily understand. Since the disease speaks through this grammar, the task of the analyst is to confront the obsessive with a complex stimulus-word that might unlock the pathology. Obsessional commands present themselves in warped, truncated form, like a disfigured telegraph message that one might only read in dreams. They are written in a code full of secret words, magical words, misspelled words, missing words, redacted words; like the grubby pieces of paper passed between spies, the enigmatic exchanges that communicate the presence of espionage. One could transmit, even write, such language without knowing what it meant. Maybe for years, maybe forever; without ever knowing whom to trust, even and perhaps especially the one who is prepared to explain it to you.

IN 1908, ROBERT WALSER WRITES about a fire in Berlin. The night is lengthening, and it is quiet in the streets. People are at home, around the table, or at a concert hall or attending the theatre, or they are hunkered over a beer talking politics. A few drunks, a hackney carriage, a woman fainting, some police—and suddenly a shout goes up, 'Fire!' The world thickens, becomes more tangible, things expand and change, people move, gravitate. Word spreads like a flame through the squares, gardens, avenues—even though several fires in one night is not unusual. The city is a forest, overgrown and half-forgotten until it catches light; it is a blind, inhuman ocean that slops in waves. You turn a corner and it's right in front of you. The street is garishly ablaze, a wounded red, the street lanterns crackle like burnt matches, the façades of buildings look like scorched paper. Voices trumpet, and you begin to run, past hackney cabs and the electric tram, until everyone stops at a point nobody knew they'd agreed to and looks back as though looking at a stage set turned into a bombsite. A thin rain of sparks and embers is falling. It covers a passing commuter train. Walser dreams of the *Thousand and One Nights*, his upturned eye exposed to the scalding particles drifting down from a rose-flecked sky. Somebody's coat catches fire, and the waves swell, flowing towards him and over him. The crowd pushes and shoves as a wind picks up. There are police on horseback and automobiles at a sudden halt, an omnibus stuffed to the cracks spills its load, and there is laughter and intimacy and heavily bated breath. New flames explode and burst and throw themselves from the windows. People come and go. Now there is water and firefighters and smoke, and the crowd is pushed back. People talk about how Berlin fires have destroyed statues and monuments, thinning out 'that old rubbish' to make room for new things, letting the traffic flow. Tiring of the spectacle, Walser leaves to find his supper. But the fire lives on behind him, eating itself with a noisy fury that sounds like language gulped down the throat. It would live on, like a bug in the city's guts.

Walser's Berlin has beer halls that are half-empty by the time evening comes, a few middle-class patrons reading their newspapers while the waiter stands by, a napkin under his arm. The world hurries along outside, moving from one place that looks like any other to another that looks like the first. A sea at nightfall. Most are already at home. The manager of the Aschinger conducts business as if running a field-camp. A picture of exhausted valour. In Berlin, a barber once casually repeated to Walser a customary saying of his: 'there is no *Kümmel* in heaven', as though flicking ash from a dying cigarette. On an electric tram you look straight ahead, and it is as if others want visible reminders of their boredom for company during the ride. The Berlin of early evening is a restless, unmoving, negligent place. When the theatre starts up, it is as if a dream of sleep calls. The theatre is a place where Germans dream under the roof, as Walser puts it. It goes on in the dark, in a hole. In front of a gaping mouth that opens as the curtain rises. Colour threatens and beguiles, some of the audience lean forward to be caught in the light, the world tilts, buildings fall and bodies sink, rifles explode and blood makes rose petals on the stage. Love happens in a garden, or there is a scream, an alleyway. Outside the moonlight is half asleep, while inside the playwright eats up scraps from the bar-room floor. In Café Bümplitz, stale tobacco fumes and a clatter of tankards accompany the musical-hall ditties of Meier, delivered with weary panache, with a don't-mind-if-I-do-ishness, Meier trouser-legging his way through the act. The Berliners laugh like they were dead, and great pleasure is had by all. All of this seemed like memory before it even happened—more than a half-century, as much as a lifetime, ago. Liesl and I could be found among the pages of those stories, each with a drink in our hand, or on their street corners in the dark, only because of Berlin's negligence—brisk and sombre and impatient and good-humoured all at once.

Unlike Paris or Rome or the other great capitals of Europe, Berlin seemed to come from nowhere. Neither out of the land nor its history. Stendhal once remarked: 'What could have possessed people to found a city in the middle of all this sand?' From the beginning, it was a rootless, inhospitable place, adrift in a spreading valley dotted with forests and marshland, blown by cold winds from the east, falling—for it is part of a sunken landform, a depression—between the Oder and the Elbe. Exposed and alone, its shifting populations etched by human conflict and human industry, Berlin grew out of a future to which one might lend the name of modernity. Despite the terrible and momentous past we ourselves recollect, it is made of events that never happened. There was no Roman occupation, no Latin credentials, no imperial seal, no claim to *romanitas*. When the Empire declined, it was the Slavs who gave Berlin its name, the first syllable deriving from the Elbe-Slav word for swamp and not, as the nineteenth-century German might have thought, from the name of the bear. When the city fell to Bonaparte, the decree issued by the Emperor introduced a new continental system founded principally on a naval blockade of the British. Prussia became merely a client state of France, switching sides during the retreat from Moscow. Berlin was no more than a counter in a larger game, and Bonaparte's famous pronouncement in 1806 attributed victory to the absence of a Frederick the Great, as if Berlin was something of an empty triumph. At the beginning of the twentieth century the German art historian Karl Scheffler—who at one time worked for Walser's Berlin publisher Bruno Cassirer—wrote that the city was always in the process of becoming. But Berlin, added Scheffler, 'never is'. The wasteland of 1945 has a curious history, holding as it does the secret memory of a place that always seems in need of a beginning. A place where no-one really belongs anymore, if they ever did, where the borders are for crossing and names are in want of a stamp or seal, where the great are already dead and remembrance struggles with its own emptiness.

Around the time I first knew her, Liesl did bits and pieces with one of the news agencies and some administrative work in connection with the Bund der Vertriebenen (BdV), the 'Assocation of the Expelled', set up in the late 1950s in the interests of the ethnic Germans who fled their homes in Central and Eastern Europe after the war. Its first president was Hans Krüger, former Nazi judge. Its founding charter, the handiwork of long-time devotees of National Socialism, made no mention of the camps and the atrocities. Now the BdV was being run by Herbert Czaja, a Christian democrat from Cieszyn. Czaja was a centrist parliamentarian and a Catholic who had volunteered for the Wehrmacht in 1942 to escape Silesia. He had refused to declare his nationality under Polish communism and believed that a reunified Germany should include the territories east of the Oder-Neisse Line, as had been the case in 1937. Liesl told me she was doing it for the money, and it was mainly by correspondence. She told me about a woman whose husband had spent ten years after the war in a Russian camp before coming home. But the couple now had a nice, modern apartment in the Hansaviertel. Anyway, she just handled some of the paperwork, it wasn't very clear to me what she did, and the salary was obviously meagre because in the mornings Liesl also washed and set hair in a small salon in one of the local neighbourhoods. She complained about the clientele, about their conversation, and about the proprietor—a loud, squat middle-aged woman who had once intimated she would pay Liesl to accompany her on a vacation to Lake Constance. In the end, she had to change jobs, not because of her boss but because the salon went up in smoke (that's probably what brought the Walser story to mind), and the business had to close. Liesl lost a good fur coat, which had been her mother's, and some work papers she had left in the cloakroom, having forgotten to post them. One of the hood dryers had not been unplugged, apparently, and it caught fire overnight. I lent her some money after that, and she began to spend more time at the university, reading the books I read and taught, writing to friends, drinking apple tea, sometimes working on an essay she had promised, sometimes taking photographs with the Leica camera she said she had found in a bar one afternoon a couple of months ago. Portraits of youth, I remember saying—snapshots of those who were almost a decade younger than her, faces that caught her eye in passing. I loved to watch her as she took them, her own face so still and composed, her hair falling in pale yellow strands that she brushed and shook away until she was still again, looking through the viewfinder like it was a keyhole. Why do you watch me? she asked. What do you think you see? training the camera on me as she spoke. My tongue burnt inside my mouth, but I told her and she smiled.

Sometime after I left Berlin, I found something in my wallet that I had written for Liesl but never given her, a poem, I suppose one would call it, on a small, folded bit of paper, written during our first weeks together, when I found I could sleep in Kreuzberg even though I'd thought I couldn't. Poetry is all too often excruciating, one's own in particular, unless of course you have no standards. I'm not sure the thing I wrote is exempt, although it's perhaps a forgivable piece of romanticism for somebody who had known hardly anything about love. I turned it over in my hands, and re-read it only because of the last line.

broken rain deepens the silence
at night, thought meets a stop
and spills itself, quietens in the warmth of you

nobody remembers the sound of rain
the breathing of love, asleep
nobody holds love like you

I wondered what I'd meant about being held. It was love, not me, that she held while she slept. But I don't think I intended a double meaning, as if love was being withheld from someone so obviously possessed by it. It's not a poem about theft. But neither is it about safekeeping exactly. It's not as if Liesl had taken my love into custody and would question it in the morning. The atmosphere of the poem is still heavy with the asymmetry of sleeping lovers—the falling apart they share as their breathing changes, even if their bodies remain entangled, orphaned by sleep. I think the poem recalls, in the memory of love, a certain experience of levitation. Held up by almost nothing, that is to say by everything intangible, warmth or the sound of rain, floating up to a height where the air gets so thin that it stops the brain, and staying there just long enough to survive. And it's true that nobody except Liesl ever made me understand that my life was like that, and that's how I think about love now.

Note ii: The obsessive is to be known by a number of characteristics. They distort the basis of their own obsessional thought-process by introducing ellipses into its primary logic. The actual manifestation of compulsive behaviour often seems bizarre because it is driven by repressions that necessarily leave gaps in the articulation of the original obsessional thinking. Missing links in the true connections between psychic materials therefore become conspicuous evidence, leaving poorly concealed clues at the scene of the crime. Other mental needs wind a knot around the neurosis, for example, a certain taste for uncertainty that tends to separate the sufferer from reality and isolate them from the world. Since obsessive behaviour is itself a formidable reaction to the possibility of resolving psychic conflict, the patient frequently avoids decision and is guilty of delay, even as they are compelled by objects or artefacts that suggest timeliness and certainty: clocks, itineraries, balance sheets. Although they often suffer from epistemophilia, compulsive types are frequently irritated by the facts. They are therefore prone to superstition, making false associations that sometimes suggest premonitory experiences. As the case of the Rat Man testifies, patients obsess over paired ideas. Through elliptical thinking, they erroneously link one psychic problem to another in ways that compound rather resolve the original difficulty—'if I were to do this (pursue a particular woman), this might happen (my father might die)'. Everything gets more distorted consequently. A sense of memory's unreliability bolsters the penchant for indecision, so that the compulsion is often accompanied by the persistent thought of having forgotten something.

The obsessive cannot decide between the love and the hatred that for Freud infuse all human attachments and must therefore somehow be resolved as part of our psychic survival. Objects of affection are at one and the same time neurotic agitants, whether loved ones or jewellery or timepieces, kindred or coins. The same goes for words. Freud even recounts the case of an obsessive *renifleur* for whom certain odours take centre stage in their neurosis. He goes so far as to speculate that an atrophied sense of smell caused by the evolutionary development of humans into an upright stance might have been responsible for distorting the natural connection between olfactory sensation and sexual instinct as it is found throughout the animal world. Getting a good sniff at things is not as easy as it once was, apparently. But it is obvious Freud thinks one can still smell a rat.

Freud's lifelong habit was to destroy the notes he made in preparation for his own published material. Once the finished article appeared in print, all the material on which it was based was discarded. As such, there are very few original manuscripts by him still in existence, much less the handwritten records from which they were derived. The Rat Man is a notable and unexplained exception to this rule. After his death, the case-notes were found among Freud's papers at his Hampstead home. Most were the daily record of the treatment that took place, although some days are missed, and the notes are written up later on. Often the documents are characterised by a word or term being inscribed vertically in the margins, as if by way of summary. This was frequently done after the fact, apparently. Indeed, as Freud's editor James Strachey points out, the chronological data surrounding the case is inconsistent, the published version failing to match up with the contents of the manuscript in several important respects, even if there are grounds to explain some of the discrepancies. Still, the suspicion is raised of another bad match. Strachey also describes the notes as being written in 'telegraphic' style. The text is littered with abbreviations, and regularly practises the exclusion of dispensable words such as pronouns. Strachey refers to the economic manner of Freud's jottings by alluding directly to 'ellipses'. Proper names are, of course, obscured or replaced by alternatives or arbitrarily selected initials. It is curious indeed that the text includes important aspects of that very same wording or grammar that typifies obsessional 'deliria'. Thinking is reduced to abbreviated language, omissions are constitutive of its elliptical style, and retrospective entries point to both sporadic lapses of memory and the punctiliousness with which it is recovered. As Strachey inadvertently suggests, the entire record reminds us of the mutilated telegraph message to which Freud himself alludes in the case study, as itself a telling figure of the distorted, truncated form of obsessional structures. But perhaps it is because they survive at all, withstanding even the most concerted effort of obliteration, that the case-notes resound so strikingly, leaving their own traces of the condition in question. As much as they document obsessive behaviour, Freud's papers form an obsessional document. Strachey concludes his introduction to the English translation of the original record of the case by averring to the uniqueness of the material as a remarkable illustration of Freud's own procedure in producing his findings. As evidence of a textual process, however, the manuscript also risks the inscription of the ailment into the analysis itself—not by recreating an impression of the illness through the practice of a certain technique, but by suggesting that the technique itself is afflicted by the sickness it hopes to treat.

The Wolf Man, that other famous case of Freud's based on the study of Russian aristocrat Sergei Pankejeff, whose obsessive religious piety took hold once early childhood had elapsed, exposed the boy's inability to dissociate Christian reverence from a recurring fascination with excrement. Three heaps of horse-dung discovered in the street involuntarily provoked the idea of the Holy Trinity. The name of God immediately triggered the thought of a dirty word like 'swine'. The boy would osculate holy images before bedtime, fervently recite prayers, and repeatedly make the sign of the cross over his own chest, yet the connection between the deity and faecal matter persisted. It stemmed, according to Freud, from a common perplexity over paternal as much as maternal birth. Before the sexual difference which gives rise to castration anxiety is recognised and accepted, it may be assumed that children are conceived and born through the anus, shared by boys and girls alike, since the alternative is even more shocking. The infant Wolf Man, however, managed to resolve the troublesome issue of Christ's toilet by reasoning that if Our Saviour could make wine out of nothing, he could equally turn food into nothing and thus avoid the humiliation of defaecating. In time, the boy's extreme religious phase softened as his own psychic relationship to his father shifted. Nevertheless, Freud tells us, it would be a mistake to assume that no lasting effects remain once the symptoms of obsessional neurosis are overcome. The Wolf Man himself never gave way to fresh thinking without making a last attempt at clinging to ideas which had lost their value. It seems especially difficult to flush away thoughts that have become waste matter—almost as if the possibility of a cure somehow depends on the contaminated material it seeks to remove. Perhaps every idea has a filthy birth, or at any rate suffers confusion about its own origins.

I WAS BEGINNING TO TIRE of the neighbourhoods around the university. It was summer and the sedentary quiet of the streets and buildings was becoming oppressive. The heat made everything open and empty. I was weary of the patterns I made, walking the pavements, crossing the roads and parks, doing some shopping or returning books, passing the same way, stopping somewhere I knew, coming back, going out again, thinking the same things as I went along, remembering things I thought I'd forgotten in the same place as before. Choosing how to dress from the few clothes I had, remembering to leave my room in a certain way so it would be like that when I returned. As if someone else would be looking at it, would be able to see it, when I wasn't there. During anxious bouts of pacing, I wondered whether I resembled the solitary figure of Robert Walser during his relentless hikes. Carl Seelig, who visited him in Herisau from the mid-1930s onwards, taking him for outings every now and again, recalled the writer's round and childlike face, cracked and bloodshot as if it had been struck by lightning, his mouth like a landed fish gaping for breath, the bottom lip bulging, the frayed collar losing its shape, the crooked tie and worn-out olive-green suit, Walser stopping occasionally with expired cigarette held under a snuffling nose to admire a meadow or a priory or a baroque house. Always without an overcoat but with the inevitable umbrella clasped in frozen, blood-blue hands. Brisk, stiff, purposeful. Seelig recounted how they would drink dark wines from Berneck or Buchberg or sparkling Bavarian beer swallowed between mouthfuls of nut crescents, talking over a lunch of meat soup and veal in mushroom cream sauce or bratwursts and mashed potato about Goethe or Stendhal or Hölderlin or Georg Büchner, or about the reading he had borrowed from the asylum library (a Smollett, for instance) or, often, Gottfried Keller. Followed by something sweet from the pastry shop washed down with a *café crème*, Robert becoming with each passing day and year less quiet and mistrustful, more voluble and light, and usually unshaven. Robert meeting him at Herisau train station in the snow or beneath an overcast sky or under leaden rainfall, sometimes riding the Appenzell railway together to Gais or Urnäsch where in 1673 (according to Seelig) the last bear in Switzerland was killed, or striding out over the fields towards St. Gallen. His brother's theatrical decorations for Reinhardt's *Tales of Hoffman*, their time together in Berlin, living in a studio with a cat named Muschi. Thomas Mann had written of him in a letter once as a 'clever child'. Kafka's recommendation of *The Tanners* and *Jakob von Gunten* to Max Brod, which Robert quickly dismissed. A farewell drink in the station restaurant at twilight; earlier that day, the happiness of clouds. For a week or so, the skies had not changed. I remembered a short story from 1910 called 'Berlin W', in which the narrator walks through parts of the city that seem to have banished poverty to the borders of open fields or to the dark interiors of tenement buildings blocked from view by stately façades, like blank faces, lining the wide avenues of the western districts. The Berliners are composed, reserved, admirable. The men are modest and unchivalrous. People stand their ground. There is no time for dreaming or gallantry or adventure, and the old seem ridiculous. A passing woman from the age of Bismarck is so severe as to be comical. A rural homesteader who has made good seems astonished by such accidental good fortune, having wandered into this place, and he gapes at the world about him in a way that utterly belies an attempt at good manners. The gardens are tidy, the architecture tends towards grandeur, monumentality. There is a certain liveliness, but it is of a healthy kind and without laughter. Walser nods at the newer world of public welfare organisations – hospitals, homes for children – as if tipping his hat; a world free from the romantic paroxysms of Frederick the Great's wars or his rococo summer palace.

Tauentzienstrasse boasts the planned elegance of a Parisian boulevard; the tree-lined Kurfürstendamm is delightful. Walser speaks of its 'calashes', by which I do not know whether he means ladies' bonnets or the horse-drawn barouche. But he finishes by putting the whole essay in a frame, a couple of pages turned into a little picture, as if Berlin W is nothing more than a coy piece of miniaturist portraiture or the stock in trade of the *feuilletonist*, a fiction composed for a spot of commerce. Walser's finale is a bit of slapstick: with animated ostentation, he bumps into the edge of his own composition before stumbling backwards out of the story. Berlin W is the stooge, impassive and straight-faced.

Liesl would come to classes, in fact she'd spend whole days at the university, but as time passed, she would come to my place less often. Outside of her studies, the neighbourhood seemed to hold little interest. So, usually, I would make the journey to her part of town, although in one sense it only lengthened the ritual monotony of my travel habits, stretching an absorbed loneliness into neatened, extended lines. Along the way, people and places were as unknown and familiar as members of a family. But there was a reassuring truthfulness about the anonymity we had in common, even if it was strange to find such reassurance in impersonal things. The outside world of my journey across Berlin always caused mixed feelings – at each step, the small relief of making one's way, the disengaged happiness and boredom of being alone and aiming for a place, sharp moments of something that felt like stage-fright on this or that corner or platform, the peculiar combination (shared by all travellers, I suspect) of an intensity and absence of thought, an interiority that was as small and overflowing and hollow as immersion in darkness or water. On this occasion, as had been the case on several others, I was so fearful of being late that I arrived far too early. But instead of going to the bar and drinking alone for an hour, I went up to her rooms. In that part of town, the distance between streets feels like a no man's land, and every street corner a border post. Like one needed passwords to communicate. Because at one time—before the city looked the way it does now (and why it does)—everyone was considered a combatant. After knocking twice, Liesl opened the door—a crack at first—and then let me in, kissing me, I remember, for longer than seemed right. She was wet and clean and beautiful. I sat by the window looking out over the street while she brought me a drink before returning to the bathroom to finish her hair. After a couple of minutes, the phone rang. I let it. Liesl didn't emerge. The ringing broke off, but then started again. I picked it up. A voice at the other end said 'Anna?' For some reason I said 'No, this is Peter, Anna's not here'. I should have said 'Do you mean Liesl?' I don't know why I replied that way, but as I did it Liesl appeared. There was a look on her face I hadn't seen. I said, stupidly, 'the phone', passing her the receiver. But the caller had rung off. 'Wrong number', I do not recall whether it was Liesl or I who said it. It must have been me. She smiled and kissed me again, as if it was nothing. Which of course it was, except I wondered why in the world anyone would say what I said. Later that evening we ate rösti and some nice cutlets and drank a bottle of crisp white wine, and I told Liesl something about my childhood in the Swiss countryside. I was born during the war in Schaffhausen, close to the German border on the northern banks of the Rhine. My father was killed in an Allied bombing raid, due to misnavigation on the part of the U.S. Army Air Forces. Everybody ignored the sirens, apparently. It was April Fool's Day, 1944. My mother never recovered, and as her decline worsened, I was put into agricultural labour as a *Verdingkinder* child. My siblings fared better. I went alone to a farm in Courtelary, ending up as far away as a village in the foothills of the Jura mountains, to dig over rough soil or carry heavy sacks of wheat or spray fertiliser from a leaking hose, dressed in thin, borrowed overalls. I remember the cold and wet and the stench. Nowhere and never was it warm. That wasn't the worst of it. Anyway, I didn't say much. Later, despite very little schooling, I was able to train for an industrial position, and from that time onwards I gradually became better qualified. But in Switzerland it's not something people talk about, a childhood like that.

A week or so later, a strange thing happened. Sitting outside a Kreuzberg café over morning coffee, someone called out to Leisl: 'Anna!' They were waving from the other side of the street. Leisl crossed over through the moving traffic, before bringing the young woman across to meet me. She said this was Ursula—I remember the name since it's more common among the Swiss—who was, apparently, someone she knew from the BdV. Laughing a little breathlessly, Liesl said that they had adopted special names for one other—Ursula called Liesl by her sister's name, the real Anna having been lost to the East after the war. For obvious reasons, she said, it was common at the BdV. The two women chatted affectionately at the table, and more drinks were ordered. At first it was all aimed at me, although within a few minutes I felt like a spectator.

The way they talked was a little adolescent, and it irritated me. Running late for an appointment, Ursula headed back up the street the same way she had come, leaving her cup unfinished. I looked across at Liesl, but she was rooting around in that bag of hers, coming up with a bright lipstick that she ran around her lips, looking hard into a compact mirror I hadn't seen before. Satisfied with her work, she snapped it shut and looked up and smiled, and we talked about something else. Perhaps it wasn't strange. I'm sure it had been a man's voice on the phone, hadn't it?—but then again the lines were often bad. Liesl didn't think to make the connection, probably she'd forgotten that call altogether. Anyway, I didn't bring it up. It seemed a small thing, and the conversation had moved on. I don't recall what we did the rest of that day, but before sleeping I remember trying to listen in the darkness for the 'Anna' that leapt in my ear on the telephone and the 'Anna' I'd heard above the traffic. But the only thing that stayed the same was the interference, a sort of low growl through which the voices came and went. Then my breathing got mixed up with the sound of a dial tone and the engine of a motorcar, and I dreamt the kind of dreams that seem to last all night. When I woke up it occurred to me that I did not ask Liesl what she called Ursula. She hadn't thought to say.

Note iii: In his short paper, 'Obsessions and Phobias: Their Psychical Mechanism and their Aetiology' (1895), written more than a decade before the Rat Man case and long before his study of the Wolf Man, which appeared just after the First World War, Freud tells us that the French philosopher and mathematician Blaise Pascal suffered from an intriguing illness. After having nearly been thrown into the Seine while riding in his coach, Pascal started to see an abyss on his left-hand side. Having described this curious affliction as the effect of a phobic response to trauma, Freud dismisses phobias in general as a basic response to fear. A phobic reaction is nothing more than an anxiety attack. Obsession is richer in the sense that it can encompass such complex emotions as doubt, remorse, and anger. It is capable of the psychic intricacies of substitution, one idea for another, which in fact establishes its primary characteristic (Freud once more attributes the peculiarity of obsessive behaviour to a *mésalliance*, this time between the subject's emotional state and the fixed idea which accompanies it—as in the case of a man so plagued by self-reproach that he feels compelled to look over his shoulder on every street corner to check he has not killed the passer-by).

But Freud's resistance to phobia as an analytic category is interesting, not least since it exhibits some of the characteristic features of unthinking recoil that suggest a phobic reaction in the first place. He deems a phobia simply a common fear subjected to exaggeration (being afraid of the night-time, of solitude, of death, of illnesses, of dangers in general, and of snakes all feature among Freud's examples); equally, however, phobias express the fear of particular circumstances that most people find untroubling (for instance, fear of open spaces or locomotion). The fact that these two seemingly contrary definitions apply to the same condition suggests Freud's difficulty in demarcating phobia (is it common or special, a heightened articulation of the norm or a peculiar departure from it, something nearly everyone or almost nobody fears?), even though such demarcation is surely the crux of that categorial distinction which determines the very title of his own paper. Accordingly, in Freud's writings from this period, the contrast between obsession and phobia is diluted by descriptions of those phobias which belong to obsessional neurosis and those which belong to anxiety neurosis; or by his admission that the presence of a phobia may be a prior indication of the onset of obsessive symptoms, which conjure up protective measures to relieve the fear. Does Freud's reaction to phobia leave an impression of fading clarity akin to the weirdly disconcerting vision of an abyss occluding one's peripheral vision? Resisting its own confinement within the schema developed by Freud, phobia careers headlong towards an altogether murkier destiny, like a coach veering off the road into the river. No wonder that the syndrome suffered by Pascal is excluded from the category-definition of obsessions and phobias with which Freud begins his paper and receives no further consideration.

For the compulsive individual, *folie du doute* brings with it anxious self-reflection about the intrusive and disruptive influence of the obsession on one's own behaviour or train of thought. However, since such pathological doubt is a symptom of the very condition it worries over, all it does—rather than to put the obsession seriously in question—is to shake one's confidence. Doubtful hesitation is a distraction—a state of distractedness—that neither protects one from nor resolves the anxiety. Perhaps Freud's uncertain categorisations of obsession suggest a case of *folie du doute*, of the kind that causes one of his own patients to re-read a letter or repeat a sum for fear of miscalculation.

Obsession is one name for the protracted endeavour of the self-treatment of illness by means of more illness. Obsession compounds anxiety in the very process of trying to confront it. How does one deal with all the fretfulness, all the disquieting unease that plagues the soul? One worries it away, taking to compulsive habits that make sure the worry is constant. Because, without them, the worries might gain an upper hand, and worry might take over. Abiding worry is the way to deal with abiding worry. The irony is probably no more lost on most obsessives than on the food addict who knows that—unlike almost any other junkie—they cannot possibly survive cold turkey. But most of the time a sense of the irony only strengthens self-doubt. I am not only sick, I know I'm sick—even if I do not know why—and I'm making myself sicker by knowing it. I know I'm making myself sicker by knowing it. Obsessional self-consciousness, as Freud points out in 'Inhibitions, Symptoms, and Anxiety' (1926), is still a symptom of repression. Nevertheless, as he observes in the same text, obsessional symptoms fall into two groups. While the more negative type—fundamental to the neurosis—involves proscriptive and precautionary measures backed up by expiation or penitence, there is also another form of obsessiveness which serves to convert the symptom into a source of gratification. The super-ego—that distorted outgrowth of an aggressive id poorly combated by an underdeveloped ego—inflicts harsh punishments on the obsessional neurotic, yet the latter mounts their defence against such cruelty through indulging the ailment. The sheer pleasure taken in collecting objects or in meticulousness or fastidious accuracy provides a way to relieve the anxiety inherent in compulsive behaviour, making use of obsession's susceptibility vis-à-vis false connection to forge ingenious associations that gratify the sufferer. Enjoy your symptom, in other words. Such capacity for neurotic pleasure — the ability to turn anxiety into its opposite — is another indication, for Freud, of the deep ambivalence and analytic richness of obsession. It adds a twist to the idea of treating illness by — or to — more illness. Especially since, by going to war with the super-ego, the quasi-egoistic self-gratification of the neurotic effectively takes arms against the libidinous desires of the id. Pleasure lined up against itself, one might say; an ego trapped in a delirious conflict where its weakness is its own defence.

❋

KARL WALSER—ABOUT WHOM I had been thinking a lot—designed stages for Max Reinhardt, the brilliant impresario and director who purchased the dilapidated Grosse Schauspielhaus (the 'Theatre of the Five Thousand') in Berlin's Friedrichstadt, across the Spree, reopening it after the First World War with a performance of Aeschylus' Oresteia. The repertoire of classical and modern drama was to be 'food for the hungry', and Reinhardt's idea was that the Schauspielhaus would become the centre of his theatrical empire. From the 1860s onwards it had been the site of a market hall before becoming a circus—the Zirkus Schumann—whose type of architecture had fascinated Reinhardt even before the war. But the trained horses had been requisitioned by the German cavalry, and crippling taxation finished the job in the Spring before the armistice. The capacious structure designed for Reinhardt by Hans Poelzig, disowned offspring of the German aristocracy, incorporated much of the circus and created the space for a vast audience. While there were good seats to be had for the right money, the interior dispensed with the theatrical balcony in favour of a spectacular commons where productions flushed with colour and ringing sound met a festive throng. The giant auditorium was to be the arena for an 'enchantment of togetherness', as Bruno Taut put it. The remnants of Zirkus Schumann provided the foundations of a magic cave. The whole thing went up like a big top in the autumn of 1919, despite the strikes and the shortage of materials. They painted it burgundy red—one critic called it a red revolution, and it was indeed the first prestige building of a young republic, a centrepiece of town planning, one might say. The stage was a full thirty metres wide, and it extended beyond the orchestra and out into a multitude lost far beneath the colossal dome. The Schauspielhaus was an expressionist Noah's ark, a vaulted sky that Poelzig (architectural advisor to the city of Dresden) had sketched on a paper napkin during, I imagine, a cheap meal. Erich Mendelsohn called it the 'experience of concrete'; Taut thought the whole edifice a consequence of Poelzig's inflationary use of the same note, the crowning tautology of his career. As much as the interior of the new theatre was conspicuously populist, the scale was imperial. As much as it anticipated the total theatre of the late twenties, the philosophical origins of Reinhardt's red castle undoubtedly predated the war, going back as far as the *architecture parlante* of Revolutionary France. The exterior had soaring pilasters, high fluted columns climaxing in symmetrical arches that corrugated the façade. Inside, the greenish foyer plunged the theatregoer into a disconcertingly continuous submarine expanse. A single central support sprouted a sheaf of ridged mouldings that spurted upwards toward the ceiling and then down over the walls, like an underwater fountain. An elephant's trunk beneath the line of the water. And one was inside it, before spilling into the amphitheatre itself, its enormous yellowish light rising like warmth towards the stalactites that hung, invisibly supported, from the ornamental ceiling—later to be pulled like decomposing, degenerate teeth when the Nazis put a false roof inside and renamed the place the 'Theatre of the People'. Late-bourgeois operettas were interrupted by the air bombings of 1945. By the time of 1961, it was in the hands of Wolfgang E. Struck, one-time member of the NSDAP who featured among Bertolt Brecht's long-standing staff after the war. Like no other building, perhaps, the Grosse Schauspielhaus dramatises twentieth-century Berlin. It is said to be afflicted by subsidence, in which case I doubt it can last much longer.

The theatre wasn't the only thing that was sinking. My research into Dürrenmatt's plays was beginning to feel like a dead weight. In my head I made a strange connection, thinking that my work was suffering, plummeting, because of Liesl. Not because she was a distraction, but because my doubts about her were somehow being punished by a self-inflicted blockage of sorts. I worried over it, and couldn't make it out, but the feeling persisted. In fact, it grew. But with it grew the uncertainty and the mistrust. Anna. Why had she been called Anna? Why had I heard that name, on the telephone and again in the café? I went over the reasons in my head, time and again: a wrong number, a pet name, a coincidence. Either one of the first two I could accept. But the third wouldn't stick and, because it wouldn't, neither would the others. The idea that one thing could be something else while being so much itself—the thought wouldn't leave me. It took different shapes, and sometimes none, but it was abiding. Until I felt I was breathing it, out and in. The idea took hold that a certain doubleness might be an essential characteristic of Liesl's, in the same way that a circus was a market hall, and a theatre was a circus. In the same way that a building could be at once imperial and revolutionary, that its politics could be so contrary and entangled. In the same way that, in a playhouse or a dream or an underground cave, one might not know for a moment whether one's head was above or beneath the water, and if by breathing one might drown. Should I confront her? What would that achieve? It would only put Liesl on her guard, and she'd be able to stabilise the ground, underpin, prevent a collapse. I'd lose the upper hand, the element of surprise in any further investigative research. But perhaps I should ask?

There might be another, simpler explanation—something harmless—that for some reason she was shy of confessing at first. No, I wouldn't ask. Bide my time, wait and see what happens, keep my eyes open. The clichés were not lost on me, and I laughed at myself, and then I'd think of something else until I started thinking about it again.

A conversation with Liesl, around that time:

—What do you know about secrets?

—What do you mean?

—I wonder what you know, Peter. For instance, when you're writing or when you read, I feel that what you love most is kept hidden. You don't seem to write about the books that are dearest to you. You don't publish on them. And when I read what you've written… well, it's not that it's enigmatic, since it's usually sparklingly clear, but it's resistant somehow.

—I suppose it's very simple. Whether I'm reading or writing something, or telling you something, whether it's me or anybody else, there's always something left unsaid. That's what language does, it causes secrets to happen. And they can't be undone, even if they're exposed, because the experience of a secret splits the truth down the middle before it even gets going.

—Yes, but you have a liking for them. That's different.

—Perhaps it's because I don't belong. The only people I have anything in common with are those I encounter on trains or in the street. Those I'll never speak to, who don't see me. We're not anything to each other. It makes me anxious but then again, I feel better somehow. And then, I suppose, there's the question of chance. Just yesterday I was walking behind some houses near my place and worrying over this and that when I noticed, over a garden wall, some small red fruits bursting from the green branches that had spread across the path. And I walked away thinking: How could I have known, even a moment ago, that today I would have the taste of raspberries in my mouth. How do you speak about that? In its entirety, I mean, when it's something which isn't of that nature.

—But you're not telling me the truth. Even now you make yourself out to be rather open, going on about trains and raspberries, but it's not openness at all. It's evasive. You have a taste for that, Peter.

—Swiss reserve. You know the story Walter Benjamin tells about Gottfried Keller, who objects so violently to Arnold Böcklin and his son twice breaking the silence over a quiet drink with just a couple of words about the weather that he rises to his feet and bellows, 'I'm not drinking with such babblers'.

—I know. It's a favourite story of yours, and you're hiding behind it again. Can't you even try to tell me what's underneath it all?

—I don't understand. You think there's something underneath? If what I've said is true, then the secret is right there on the surface, hiding in plain sight, or else its greatest trick is to convince you it ever existed in the first place. It's like a half-forgotten memory of something that never happened.

—That's your answer to everything. What didn't happen, Peter?

—I don't know exactly.

—Did it not happen in Courtelary, or was it before then?

—...

—I'm sorry.

—Why do you want to know about secrets, anyway?

—I want to know what they mean.

—I don't know what they mean, Liesl.
—I think they mean you love something.

The whole exchange was bathed in laughter and smiles. And then we got on to something else. But I felt she wasn't so much asking as trying to tell me something.

For some reason I felt a compulsion to make a list of Liesl's reading habits, since they were particular:

1. When Liesl turned the page of a book, she would turn the page again, to look at the rear side of it. She did not seem to read any of the words particularly but glanced across the surface of the writing as if to make sure that nothing unexpected was there. Each time it was very quick, and afterwards she would settle herself, shifting her weight in her seat or titling her head at a new angle to concentrate, which she did intently until she was at the end of the page. Then, when she'd finished, she would turn it over, and over again, then back. And she'd settle herself again. It was a habit Liesl maintained without fail, at least in my experience, but she seemed unaware she was doing it.
2. To mark a page, Liesl would neither turn down a corner nor make an insertion of any kind into the book (a torn strip of paper, say). Instead, she would take a separate sheet, or more likely an old envelope or an unused postcard from that bag of hers and make a note of the page number together with a scrawled comment that anybody else would find illegible. And then, folded, it would go back into the rubble, the wreckage and detritus that she carried around with her. Now that I think of it, I never saw her retrieve those notes she scribbled down or make any use of them.
3. Needless to say, Liesl would never write in a book, and, if anybody else ever did, you could see her wince

the way people do in the presence of bad table manners.
4. When she paused reading, Liesl would always leave a book face down on the table. At rest, the book was always closed, it was never left spread apart, covers up, like a squashed tent. It was as though whatever she took from a book was extracted invisibly, and the object itself was left intact, like a radio that had been switched off or a piece of clothing drying in the sun.
5. Sometimes Liesl would hold a book in one hand, at arm's length, as if inspecting rather than reading it. Always with a curious squint. Sometimes, as I mentioned, she would grip a book tightly in both hands as if it were a steering wheel, pressing her back hard into the seat as if to cope with the velocity.
6. I never saw Liesl curl up, as the phrase goes, with a book.
7. When Liesl spoke about a book she was reading, she rarely said what she thought of it, but always talked instead in terms of what you – what I – might think of it.
8. She preferred to carry a book in the deep pockets of her coat.
9. If Liesl was reading on a bus or a train, and wanted to rest, she would not leave the book in her lap but place it on the next seat, unless it was occupied, in which case she would put it back in her pocket and, if possible, place the folded coat in a luggage rack.
10. Liesl disliked borrowing or lending books, but would sometimes break the rule where I was concerned.

Note iv: In 'Inhibitions, Symptoms and Anxiety' Freud detects two specific techniques that occur in the formation of obsessive symptoms. The first he describes as 'undoing what has been done'—which involves a desire not only to reverse the consequences of some previous occurrence, but to erase the past entirely. Undoing-what-has-been-done aspires to the ingenuity of a magician's disappearing act, where the audience can fathom neither the absence of the object nor the trick itself (this is one reason Freud gives as to why the obsessional neurosis is particularly recalcitrant to analysis). Whereas in normal behaviour a person can effectively regard an event as having not taken place in the sense of ignoring its implications, an obsessive individual will actively seek to obliterate it—often by means of some ritual or ceremonial device. It is as if the sufferer is incapable of everyday amnesia. Freud does not give an example of this behaviour, before moving on to the second practice adopted by compulsive types, which he labels 'isolation'. The obsessive neurotic will defend against the return of repressed material through recourse to an intense form of concentration that serves to block it out. Again, because it seems impossible simply to forget or ignore unwanted ideas or experiences, they are instead deprived of their affect. Disturbing connections in the thought-process are wilfully interrupted, worrisome associations are subjected to isolating separations. Ambivalence is combated by an intensity of focus and discipline; every particle of thinking is atomised.

A corollary of this activity is a deep resistance to touching on the part of the obsessive individual. The avoidance of contact is inherent in the symptomatic techniques of 'undoing' and 'isolation'; more specifically, neurotic behaviour seeks defence against the cathexes – whether aggressive or loving – through which barriers are breached and distance is overcome. Whether stroke or strike, the obsessive-compulsive flinches from every touch. They dwell instead in a land of false connections designed to avoid contact with what is real. Ideas as much as bodies must not touch one other, memories must not even brush fingertips. The merest intimacy sparks a prolonged and exhaustive washing of hands. The loneliness of obsession is absolute in this regard. And yet in contrast to animal phobias, say, where the sense of danger is largely externalised, obsessional anxiety is mainly an internal affair: as close to oneself as possible, in fact. Freud uses the term 'endo-psychic'. Further on in the text, he endeavours to determine the nature of anxiety by distinguishing its principal characteristics in relation to similar states such as mourning or pain. A striking feature of anxiety, according to Freud, is that it responds to non-present danger (consequently it is an inexpedient reaction to immediate threat). Perhaps the prototype for anxious feeling is therefore the trauma of birth – Freud inherits this idea from Otto Rank but disputes his view – which is historically original for each individual as much as it seems psychologically irretrievable. Birth is absolutely initial – the very advent of presence – and yet the experience is unrecoverably absent, hence for Rank it provides not merely a prime example but the founding conditions of anxiety. The source of anxiety is as far away as possible, even if it is felt as closely as can be.

It seems quite natural, says Freud, that a four-year-old girl would shed tears over a lost doll, or that a six-year-old would cry when told off by her teacher, or that a sixteen-year-old would despair when rejected by her first boyfriend. But it seems equally natural that these small agonies fade in time. Even as a grown adult, meanwhile, the neurotic will howl over a broken trinket. The smallest thing, the most petty of things, triggers a desperate affect, as though the tiniest dredge might bring up an entire sea bed. The neurotic never seems to grow out of it, they cannot get over it. Imagine how painful that is—not only to suffer the terrors of childhood long into maturity, but to have them colour and contaminate and compel all the hurt and loss and fear and disappointment and grief that everybody must endure throughout a lifetime. Imagine going through all of that with the same feelings one had, so long ago now, when one thought a mother's most precious ornament had been broken. Knowing those feelings can come back at any moment, without warning and on endless repeat, connecting the oldest, most abiding suffering with an infantile intensity of pain. Trapped in a past that is lost, terrified like a bereaved child left alone in the darkness.

Anxiety is all about expectation. But indefinite expectation, expectation in want of a definite object. Yearning fear at the prospect of the unknown, neurotic anticipation of an impending future that fills and empties the present as if it were the hollowest of nights. Helplessness. A weak sense of foreboding which repeats the terrible expectation it hopes to ward off. The child who wakes from night terrors holds their breath in the dark, literally scared stiff, listening so intently that they wonder if the sound of their listening will give them away.

WHEN HE FLED GERMANY FOR AMERICA in 1938, Mies van der Rohe—whose most famous aphorism was perhaps 'God is in the details'—left Lilly Reich to manage his affairs, and it is said she saved thousands of his drawings from likely destruction by the Nazis. On his invitation Lilly had taught at the Bauhaus in the early thirties, just before it had been forced to close. More than a decade earlier, she had been the first woman to be elected to the Board of the Deutscher Werkbund. She was an embroiderer who had begun at the Vienna workshop of Josef Hoffman before returning to her home city of Berlin in 1911 to become a member of the Werkbund, from whence she collaborated on the interior design of the Haus der Frau, exhibited in Cologne the year the war started. The latter she spent as a seamstress. Lilly met Mies in the mid-twenties in Frankfurt, where she had been designing for trade fairs. For many years they were constant companions. She visited him in Chicago in 1939 but returned to spend the war in Germany—the last years of it in forced labour, dying just a short period afterwards. They worked together on the famous Barcelona Chair for the International Exposition of 1929—it is said the design was really hers—made for Spanish royalty but modelled on the *sella curulis*, the seat of Roman power. Hardly anyone remembers Lilly now, although her contribution to modern textiles and furniture was considerable and lasting. Her great triumphs included the interior of the celebrated Tugendhat House in Brno, which won Mies many plaudits, and the *Wohnraum in Spiegelglas*, the sparest of living rooms geometrically apportioned by rectangular uprights of mirrored panelling. Better than anyone, Lilly understood the architecture of interior design, the elegance and simplicity of unornamented form, the minimality required if spatial division was to acquire a modern sense of grandeur. Like Karl Walser, she knew how to stage space. That hundreds upon hundreds of the plans and sections drafted by Mies should have emerged from the devastated cartography of a Germany that Lilly did not survive is a terrible irony. Germany's fate was to suffer a type of partition that was altogether different, completely unrecognisable in comparison to her artistic vision—which was, among other things, deceptively modest yet acutely open and hospitable. Instead of lines that separated in order to unify, her country succumbed to borders made less to be crossed than double-crossed. Contaminated edges which, try as one might, it is impossible to avoid touching, because they have already forfeited the clarity that would determine their frontiers or isolate their contours. It is not only that one recoils from them, since that is impossible; their contact is estranging. I have always thought that works of art, properly speaking, do not exist at the limits of language but rather—by overwhelming them—make it possible. That is the kind of frontline which, it seems to me, Berlin lacks. That is what's missing.

The Wall isn't a frontline, it's a stand-in for the absence of one. Around the old Potsdamer Platz, disused tracks disappear into it and go nowhere. If Lilly's furniture was characteristically tubular in its modernism, the lines that define the city—even when they look straight—are as circuitous as Berlin's ring road yet more knotted, doubling back to get caught up in themselves like barbed wire. In its broadest sense, the architecture of Berlin has been closely connected to the historical administration of traffic. This is true not only of the post-war period, but for much of the twentieth century. In Walser's little story about a spreading fire at night, the crowd applauds a future where streets are uncluttered by monumental debris. The colour-tone of the city is established by buildings but also by roads and the vast paraphernalia of roads. The trams made way for motor vehicles long ago. Walter Ruttman's *Sinfonie der Grosstadt* (1927) is a case in point: the tempo of the film is positively automotive; the driving is reckless and high-speed and in need of conducting by a policeman's baton. Statisticians of the inter-war years created an entire industry from the rising casualties. Urban planning fed off it. But Gottfried Feder, Berlin civil engineer and co-founder of the German Workers Party (the precursor of the NSDAP) considered the roads of the metropolises a raging inferno that might consume the German *Volk*. Nazis were more ambitious, I guess, than to see traffic as the opportunity for law enforcement. But traffic technologies, so to speak, nonetheless convey certain fascistic aspects of modernity (Rudolf Hess was much more glowing about the *autobahns* as an expression of national culture), even if the backlash against the motor car—as the example of Gottfried Feder suggests—does not simply put them into reverse. Public transport, the U-Bahn in particular, may well be the nervous sinew of the city, but the car is the pulse. After the First World War, a rationalised traffic system was thought of by many as the key to a modern, integrated, and revived Germany. The land was a body that could be prosthetically altered by surgical cuts beneath the skin, by new limbs constructed across the country's formidable physique. New arteries could be sown into its flesh. Hence the psychic ambivalence of the Hitlerists, whose relation to monstrosity was complex. At any rate, travel in Berlin nowadays is not what was hoped for in the 1920s and 30s. I'm avoiding thinking about Liesl.

—Why are you writing about Dürrenmatt?
—You know why. Swiss author. Revival of post-war German drama. The ghosts of religion and the trauma of war. Writes and paints. The Olten Group, Max Frisch. The Zürich cabaret. The radio plays of the 1950s.
—Yes, thank you for the potted biography. You know what I'm asking. His politics.
—You're asking about his credentials. Left the Schweizerischer Schriftstellerverein with the others because Zermatten translated the anti-communist Civil Defence Book for the Swiss French. That's something. And Epic Theatre, of course.
—Brecht never joined the Party.
—He supported the State against the uprising in '53.
—Have you read '*Die Lösung*'?
—I thought we were talking about Dürrenmatt?
—I know, but my point is that Brecht gave public assurance of his solidarity and suggested support for the military action and then just months later he writes a bitter satirical poem about the government's repression of the people. It says everything about a Weimar experimentalist. Cheap iconoclasm.
—Is satirical the right word? Are any of those the right words? Anyway, you're being provocative.
—And you're being evasive again.
—...
—You know about Brecht's productions at Reinhardt's *Deutsches Theater* in the twenties?
—Yes.
—Just helping you with your love of complication.
—You'll be decrying formalism next. Liesl, when you're unreconstructed like this, it's a pantomime.

All done with smiles and laughter. I remember we kept going—the idea of dramatic fate, the tradition of the morality play, absurdist theatre—it seemed as if to keep the political bait on the line. I knew she was being playful, but I also understood she wasn't exactly joking. I remember wanting to withdraw into the Dürrenmatt, to reclaim it privately—not that I loved the writing, but because of my research—yet at the same time feeling piqued because I knew what Liesl would think about that. I didn't want her looking at that.

Note v: In early 1907, for the first time in a decade, Freud returned to the question of obsessional neurosis, further elaborating some of the psychic characteristics that would appear in the case history of the Rat Man, whose treatment he had not yet begun. The paper, read at a meeting of the Viennese Psycho-Analytical Society at which Jung was present for the first time, may be seen as an introductory foray into the psychology of religion. Freud describes the resemblance between obsessive ceremonial and pious ritual. The fastidious performance of obsessional behaviour is obviously akin to the observance of sacred rites. Each relies on painstaking attention to detail, a highly structured orderliness of procedure, an intensely conscientious disciplining of one's habits, and a severe intolerance of deviation or interruption. Both also resort to frequently bizarre embellishments of everyday actions, to heighten symbolic significance while preserving the enigmatic meaning of the ceremony. Prohibition, remorse, temptation, penitence, a predeterminative sense of expectation—such feelings dominate the mind of the neurotic as much as the believer. They reflect the protective wishes for which idolatry was invented, like an insurance policy whose premium must regularly be paid.

While most religious observances include elements of a public and communal nature, however, the practice of obsessional neurosis is almost always a solitary matter. Indeed, the sufferer often succumbs to compulsive ceremonial behaviour in private while still being able to conduct their social life in a way that is unaffected by the illness. Perhaps, after all, it is in the personality of religion to enjoy a taste for secrets. Be that as it may, Freud likens the devotion of obsessive types to the fabled Mélusine, whose mermaid-like figure must remain hidden from view. The strange marvels of neurotic compulsion are always veiled; its rites constitute an observance without witness, an affair that might never have happened. A mystery of the kind which goes to the very heart, perhaps, of the sacred.

Maybe due to false decorum, a propriety of manners that is all but obsolete and hence prone to irony, Freud remarks that the comparison between religion and neurosis is obviously sacrilegious. In its tragi-comic way, needless to say, obsession merely travesties reverent belief. But Freud is quick to subvert his own rather manufactured etiquette. Since obsessional behaviour is never unjustified or unmotivated, it precisely shares with religion the compulsion to make symbolic representations of significance. Indeed, an affinity between the unconscious origins of obsessive behaviour and a devotional love of sacred mysteries is not lost on Freud; in both cases, pious observance outranks penetrating comprehension of one's god. Faith triumphs over knowledge. Towards the end of his paper, Freud even feels encouraged to speculate, not only that obsessive individuals are especially prone to religious belief, but that obsessional neurosis may be a pathological counterpart in the formation of religions themselves, a psychical supplement without which they cannot do. And in the religious sphere as in the field of mental illness, the mechanism of psychical displacement is of crucial importance—meaning shifts from what is actually significant to a diminuted substitute, an apparently trivial detail, a petty ceremony. By this means, what is small becomes momentous. But the small is, of course, as much an ambivalent bedfellow as an ardent lover, because it is the product of a *mésalliance*. Its offspring, in fact. To be precise, an abused child.*

All of which would imply that significance itself—for which religious meaning is obviously prototypical—proceeds based on a false connection. In his 1962–63 seminar, under the general heading of Anxiety, Jacques Lacan—feted as the inheritor of Freud—insists on the following: what is not simply quintessentially human, but quintessentially signifying, is the act of laying false traces with the purpose of making others believe they are false. Animals, he says, lay false traces all the time. But, unlike humans, they do not lay them in the hope or expectation that they will be taken for false. When a trace has been made to be taken for a false trace, Lacan concludes, we know that there is a speaking subject. The false trace that is made to be taken as false is perhaps the very issue of psychoanalysis.

* It should be noted that Peter Müller penned a series of short and disconcerting essays on the topic of the 'small', which came to light just after his death, in which he wrote about tics, toys, puppets, the invention of the paper clip, little jokes, and child abuse. It was as if, for Müller, the 'small' unlocked whole worlds: art, culture, psychology, perhaps even the legacy of the European twentieth century—at least insofar as his own life was shaped and stricken by such momentous forces. The reader will notice that the word itself arises many times in the present text. (S.K.)

✵

ANNA. I'D BEEN REREADING *Der grüne Heinrich* and had forgotten that one of the two loves of Keller's hero is called Anna. It wasn't a personal favourite of mine, that book, as it had been of Robert Walser. I have a professional interest, of course, in the *Bildungsroman* as the handiwork of German literary criticism or, to be more exact, the historical product of European aesthetics. The extensive revision of *Green Henry* which culminated in the 1879 version, published almost a quarter of a century after the original, is an enormous source of interest in that regard. But now I came to think of it, 'Anna' as the name for a love that comes behind or before another—did that idea echo across the span of days dividing a wrong number from a chance meeting? Is that the reason I came to dwell on it? In Keller's novel, Anna represents a virtue to which there is more than meets the eye—Judith being the older, more sensual and knowing, at times more visceral expression of the protagonist's longing—since the double and duplicitous desire of the central character inscribes uncomfortable questions about the sexual politics of innocence and experience into the aesthetic project of the *Bildungsroman*. And since the whole novel is an autobiographical invention on Keller's part, a certain line inevitably runs from Heinrich to the author to the male reader, a connection in which collusion is difficult to avoid. I can scarcely remember now whether I restarted *Green Henry* before or after my misgivings about Liesl took hold. I doubt my own memory on that point.

Chapter two of the second part of the book is titled 'Judith and Anna'. Heinrich is up in the mountains, fawning over an idealised image of Anna. In fact, it has taken possession of him, and he delights in the expectation of their next meeting, although mention of the delicate figure of the schoolmaster's little daughter adds a delicious taste of shame to the mix of ingredients. But the mountain path takes him past Judith's door, into whose hymn book he has slipped pictures of little garlands of flowers painted at her request, accompanied by a witty motto or by verses printed on to the wrappings of bon-bons that have long since been eaten. One woman is duly taken in default of another, without any sense of inconstancy. In the presence of the full bloom of womanhood, writes Keller, Heinrich is able to indulge his thoughts of the tender bud. In the mornings, Judith would comb her hair, which fell to her hips when loose, and as a tease Heinrich would play with it, Judith's hands resting obediently in her lap. When they are alone, he starts to pull it loose himself, even if it is already bound up. One evening, coming away from the mountain, he finds Judith washing salad leaves and vegetables in the spring that runs behind her house. He holds her hands under the clear stream, washing and rubbing them as one might a child's, trickling drops of cold water on to her neck and finally splashing some in her face. Until she takes his head and holds it tightly in her lap, smacking it until the wished-for punishment becomes too severe and Heinrich pulls away, taking hold of Judith's head in revenge. A hard, breathless struggle follows, after which both are gasping and flushed, his arms wound around her white neck. Spent, he thinks again of Anna. The image of her purity, of course, is the very height of the obscenity of his thoughts. Anna. Was Liesl really my Anna? Was that why a second name, spoken twice, could not be overlooked as a coincidence? Liesl was nothing like her. But the doubts I was having—if I were to dream them, would I find myself by a stream in the mountains, desperately clenching at the throat of a woman? It's not Judith, it's Anna who's the figure of the double – but of Keller's double, Heinrich. Shame is what might be called a longing for innocence after the violence. That's what deceit is. And one needs to know where to look for it.

Note vi: In 'Mourning and Melancholia" (1917) Freud suggests that, while both grieving and melancholy result in a twofold separation that combines loss of interest in the world with a weakening of the capacity for love, melancholia is frequently prolonged beyond a period of mourning because the object of loss is not known in the same way. Mourning is the process of accepting the passing of a particular someone, but melancholia sets in when the sufferer does not know *what*, even if they know *whom*, has been lost. The consequent predicament traps the melancholic in a sort of psychic vicious circle. Melancholics are in addition liable to mania, resulting in various states of elation—undue yet energetic joyfulness, triumphalism, excitability, or intoxication—which offer a sense of freedom and relief from the moribund feelings that persistently ail and subdue them in frequently obscure ways. Mania is obviously not unproblematic, however, as a protective reaction to the self-destructiveness that melancholy invites.

In 'The Ego and the Id' (1923), Freud makes a distinction between the deep capacity for self-harm caused by melancholia and the limits of the suffering experienced by obsessional neurotics. In the former case, the super-ego enjoys a stranglehold over the subject's ego that is so absolute it risks the free reign of the death-instinct. Mania is the only recourse left to its victim, who in seeking a reprieve from self-destructive feelings resorts to a hyperintense counter-symptom. In contrast, the reproaches of conscience that afflict the compulsive type of person seem to be accompanied by a relative degree of immunity from suicidal thoughts. This is because, unlike the melancholic, the obsessional neurotic is able to retain the 'object' (presumably even through the processes of substitution) and aggress against rather than succumb to it as an unknown quantity. Destructiveness is thereby directed at the 'object' rather than the 'self'. Self-reproach comes when the super-ego rails against the neurotic's ego precisely because the aggressivity of the id has been unleashed. But Freud implies that this provides the opportunity for a kind of ego-workout, a training opportunity for it to build better defences against super-ego and id alike—to build psychic muscle rather than succumb to the atrophying effects of melancholia. In other words, whereas the melancholic individual drifts towards death, the obsessive person learns survival through their neurosis. It appears obsession is the thing that does not despatch you—what does not destroy you—in the Nietzschean sense of making you stronger. From the school of life that teaches war. Melancholy, meanwhile, encourages a pacifism that kills.

One can only speculate—at the limits of Freudianism—what causes the melancholic to live on, and what makes the obsessional neurotic call it a day. After all, if Freud found it more difficult than he first imagined to confidently distinguish phobia and obsessions (and in the early psychoanalytic publications of the 1890s a number of references to 'mixed' neuroses suggest that psychic conditions may sometimes overlap), then who is to say that the destructiveness of melancholy—against which mania provides a modicum of relief—and the resilience of compulsive neurosis—which is itself prone to violent attack on every front—are immune from mutual contact? In 1895, concluding his paper on anxiety neuroses, Freud comments that anxious symptoms often combine with hysteria, obsession or melancholia. This does not militate against the distinctiveness of each complaint, but nevertheless an interspersed neurosis must be acknowledged as evidence of the admixture of several specific aetiologies, in other words of a multiple and interconnecting number of causes. At any rate, it is certainly true that both melancholy and obsession have their defensive reflexes but that each is pitted in circumstances fraught with risk. Each is assailed by something at once inside and outside itself. Something like a *mauvaise connexion* as much as a *mésalliance*, perhaps, due to interference on the line – maybe of the type you read about in a cold war spy novel.

I REALISED I WAS TURNING MYSELF into a character in a book. What good was that to anybody? It would make Liesl laugh, wouldn't it, if I told her? In my room at night, it was the scale of the darkness that mattered, since I slept badly and fought for sleep and could tell from the depth of the light that came from outside what time it was, more or less exactly, even with my eyes closed. I had no clock by the bedside because knowing the time made everything worse, but still the window made sure I knew. A silvery blue bled into black and I knew time was draining away by the half or quarter hour, until at last the density of light was too much and I gave up. And then I slept while ribbons of weightless yellow wound themselves around the bookcase or the table like blind tongues, dragging them across the room. For a game, I would lie awake and list all the Annas I knew: Anna O., who Breuer described as having 'absences', Anna Freud, Karenina—I was trying as much to bore as ridicule myself, and sometimes I fell asleep doing it. Anna O., fell ill at twenty-one years old (1880). Moderately severe neuropathic heredity, but parents and earlier childhood normal, unremarkable. Notably intelligent. Could digest 'solid mental pabulum'. Therefore unsuggestible. The element of sexuality undeveloped in her. Day-dreamt as if in a 'private theatre'. The manifest illness (1880–82): paraphasia, severe disturbances of vision, a squint, paresis of neck muscles, paralytic contractures, somnambulism. Father's death due to peripleuritic abscess in April 1881. Onset of *tussis nervosa* (nervous cough), exacerbated by dancing music. Sometimes she thought the walls were falling over. If objects in her bedroom were moved, would complain of having 'lost' time.

Hallucinations of black snakes in her hair or at her fingertips. Inability to conjugate verbs, or to use definite or indefinite article: atoms of near-unintelligible speech. Amnesiac confusion of European languages. Withdrawal manifested by habitual deafness. During treatment, described her own talking cure as 'chimney sweeping'. 5 grammes of chloral to induce sleep. Freud's description of her *condition seconde* or 'double conscience'. Anna O.'s 'bad self', as she described it.

I'd oversleep. Opening my eyes, the room was outspread and bright and reproachful. I don't know why I didn't close the blinds fully, perhaps another kind of fearfulness. I felt as though I couldn't move. But I'd be on time to teach my class, Dürrenmatt or Büchner or Herman Hesse, and then some coffee with the students and perhaps Liesl would be there.

—A student movement like the 68ers couldn't resurface after everything that's happened. Not in that form.

—Well, there are still Nazis in West Germany, Peter, there are still nuclear weapons, capital still works the way it does, the issues haven't gone away.

—You had a mass sit-in at Freie Universität two years before they tried to kill Rudi Dutschke, the year before they shot Benno Ohnesorg here in Berlin. But not after Baader-Meinhof.

—The reasons are different. The student groups splintered, the APO didn't hold, how could it?

—Because people radicalised. They went too far. They went underground. They burned department stores. You had everything that came after the May offensive in '72. It just became suicidal and went nowhere.

—But Peter…

—I know what you're going to say. Maybe we should just drop it. They say the Stasi had a hand in Ohnesorg and

maybe Dutschke too.
—I thought we were dropping it?

I had a full afternoon of tutorials but was heading up to Liesl later that evening. Kotti was greying against the evening sun, and beneath tree-lined streets the signs were lit for piyaz and kofte and watch repairs. Little movie theatres and bars were opening up, and the air smelled of tobacco smoke and petrol. Motorbikes wove in and out of the traffic. Flat-fronted buildings rose high above street cafés, their interiors spiced with sweat and caffeine and mint and patchouli. An hour ago, it had rained. Since I had some time to spare, I found a place and ordered some tea and sat down to read an article for *October* (which was very new at that time) since I'd agreed to report on it. I took the paper out of my bag and started making notes, taking sips from a slim-waisted crimson glass while pencilling comments in the margins. I could compress words and sentences into a very small hand, so that my writing crocodiled around the edges of the text, making a tailback from the corners, and turning left or right at the bottom or top of the page into a clear slip lane above or underneath. I never wrote on the reverse of the single-sided typed submissions sent me by academic journals, even though it wasn't customary for me to return scripts with the report. It was a tiny pleasure of mine. The rain started again suddenly, blotching the ink, and looking up at the sky I saw Liesl across the road, heading away from me, just beyond the distance where I could call out her name. She wore a new blue dress. I stuffed the essay back in my bag, left some money on the table, making sure to point it out to the waiter, and made after her. I suppose I'm somebody who wouldn't raise their voice in the street, so I quickened my pace to catch her up. As I hurried along, I had the oddest feeling that the man in front of me was following Liesl just as I was. I don't know why, perhaps it was because each of his movements echoed mine, or mine his, as he wove in and out of the people walking towards or away from both of us. I remember thinking it felt like formation flying during a raid. Up ahead Liesl turned a corner, and after a moment so did he. I hung back a little but followed them into a side street where Liesl stepped into a doorway by a small shopfront, disappearing up a staircase when the door opened. The man broke his stride, stopped, crossed over the road and vanished into an alleyway between two of the buildings opposite. I turned on my heels, walked twenty yards back up the street, and waited. I waited for fifteen minutes. Liesl re-emerged and took to the pavement, heading in the direction of her place. The man was nowhere to be seen. I didn't follow her. Instead, I made my way towards the café I had just left—I don't know why, since I didn't go in but instead circled back to follow my own footsteps, past the little shopfront and the alley, before going on to Liesl's. I've just got back, she said, you must have followed me up the stairs. She was laughing and she kissed me, as she always did, in a way that meant I could taste her mouth, which tasted of caviar or gunmetal or something I couldn't recognise. I didn't tell her what just happened. And then everything was the same, we talked, and we went out for something to eat, and had too much to drink and I mentioned the dress and we argued about a new shirt I'd bought, which she said made me look too old. I stayed at hers, which was something of a rarity, and left in bright sunshine early the next day thinking that Kotti was getting worse, and I didn't want to come back for a while. And I felt like a character in a book.

How Liesl walked: forwards, with purpose, shoulders back, hair falling to nearly the small of her back, moving as she swayed, on heels, her ankles naked, slender, one hand on her shoulder bag, maybe one in the pocket of her coat, or falling free, she moved like a proud animal, a woman who had never been a child, each step an intent expression of a movement that seemed beyond doubt, not looking back, absorbed in movement, everything around her drawn into the passage she made, as if the word carriage had been invented for her. Her hips pushing at the world. My heart beating. Vitally tall, irrespective of height, whether hers or anybody else's. As straight and as upright as you could be. Sometimes, with hair pinned, her bare neck like stripped bone or an alpine pass, pure wordless movement, stature in flight. Walking as the expression of a distance that encloses everything within itself. Memory losing breath in the slipstream of her. As if she was already there, wherever she was going. Inhuman grace, to borrow some words from Kleist, passing through infinity. That's how she walked.

Note vii: In 'A Short Account of Psycho-Analysis', written during the early 1920s, Freud reflects on the impetus given by the creative mind to wish-fulfilment. Substitution is of course at the imaginative heart of deriving satisfaction from unearthed desires. This exchange of material, transiting from unconscious life to inventive consciousness, is how creation converts repression into art, literature, and myth. Artistic realisation is like a dream-work, and the heightened emotional impact of what is often a dramatic transformation connects the work of the artist with the behaviour of a neurotic.

One of Freud's most famous examples of obsessional neurosis is found in his study of Leonardo da Vinci (1910), the stimulus for which was apparently his recent treatment of the condition in a patient. Freud paints Leonardo as an epistemophiliac, compelled by a neurotic thirst for knowledge that sublimates unreconciled sexual instincts. Boundless curiosity, observes Freud, implies only a continual deferral of the question that cannot be asked; such curiosity is converted into prolonged research investigations, the complexity of which often reflects the distortion implied by avoidance of the actual problem that has undergone repression in the first place. That is how obsessional thinking forms knowledge of the world, how it broods compulsively over the intelligence at hand. Like the secret service—at once powerfully driven, microscopically engaged, and increasingly twisted out of shape. As clear-cut answers retreat towards an ever-receding horizon, scrutiny intensifies, the investigation deepens, a stewed atmosphere sets in. The pedantry of Leonardo's household ledger suggests a meticulous computation of accounts, as apparently inconcludable as it is fastidious. Trying to make everything tally—the price of silver brocade and crimson velvet trim, braid, buttons, and stockings to dress an absconded pupil, the cost of his mother's funeral casket and candles—becomes a labyrinthine task without foreseeable end. And, just as is the case in a spy story, it is those closest to Leonardo who are implicated in an obscure economy of debt, deceit, and sudden disappearance. All of which is accompanied, says Freud, by a warped sense of drama which corresponds to the heightened emotional state of obsessional neurosis. Leonardo's accounts are narrated with the intensity, not just of a personal diary, but of a psychological novel. Remnants of Leonardo's hidden desires cling to this interminable reckoning-in-secret, funded by an abiding sense of treachery and betrayal—including his own, although that is hardly acknowledged, because of course Freud's da Vinci is a double-agent who has traded poor substitutes for the real thing.

Needless to say, the connection between homosexuality and espionage is an enduring feature of the cold war imagination. It is said that totalitarian regimes were never averse to cultivating this connection, exploiting homosexuals for their contacts (who, in turn, might readily be manipulated because of their own closet activities) while benefiting from a certain aptitude for clandestinism on the part of such agents. Honeytraps and blackmail are usually the counterpart of this supposed talent for covertness, as the case of British civil servant and KGB spy John Vassal amply demonstrated. Whether such circumstances have proven entirely effective insofar as the authorities are concerned—undoubtedly the duplicity of spies is a matter of constant anxiety, bordering on paranoia, as much as it is a literal expectation—the idea of the undercover homosexual as an ambivalent resource risks naturalising assumptions about the fraudulence and dishonesty inherent in a so-called sexual deviant, a queer 'other'. From Christopher Marlowe to Guy Burgess, the idea of the double-agent crossing sexuality and politics is in danger of being trite. Whether an Elizabethan playwright or Cambridge historian turned diplomat, it is interesting that such figures are commonly associated with the arts rather than the sciences — Leonardo, as Freud himself points out, is thought of in the public mind foremost as a painter, Freud's Leonardo being the one whose cradle-dream was of a vulture's tail knocking against his open lips. Perhaps it is creativity — of a particular kind, at any rate — which inspires mistrust. Obsessional inventiveness is probably a case in point, not least because it is prone to hesitation and self-doubt (but also sly, defensive aggression) of the kind that fuels *la guerre froide.*

I had been thinking about the thrust that happens after a blast. Not just the blast, which throws itself out with such force that the aether becomes insanely compacted, compressed particles of air percussing with the velocity of light. And not just the shock waves of pure energy that invisibly cut through tissue or crush organs or burn minds without trace. Not the shrapnel or the fire and heat. I'd been thinking about the vacuum that forms behind that madly dense outward thrust of air. In an instant it refills itself with the surrounding atmosphere, wrenching at the splinters of matter in supersonic flight across the universe, pulling them back in. As if calling them home, in their absolute brokenness, their reduction to sheer flecks of existence, but calling them back to a nothingness. A blast catapults but also magnetises, whether the falling of a bomb or a war itself, as if one were a clown in a silent comedy with his braces caught in the door. Like Benjamin's Angel of History, his eyes staring, mouth open, wings spread, face turned to the past, wreckage upon wreckage hurled at his feet by a single catastrophe. The angel yearns for the dead to live, for what is smashed to become whole again. But a storm blows from Paradise, catching his wings, and he is thrown into a future he cannot see, since his back is turned to it. In the passage in question, Benjamin is talking about a painting by Paul Klee, *Angelus Novus*, but the epigram for the 'Theses on the Philosophy of History' comes from a poem by Scholem: 'My wing is ready for flight, I would like to turn back, If I stayed timeless time, I would have little luck'. Benjamin says, bitterly, that the storm—the blast—is what we call progress.

It struck me that those of us born during the war and those of us born afterwards—those of us who weren't really there—are no less than angels. But just as the storm catches them, a vacuum drags at our wings. We have been hurled out with such incomparable violence but with that same violence seized at the edges of what is now nothing, blinded by the swirling shards of dust it sucks down, our lungs blasted, suffocating, invisible shocks coursing through bone and flesh like water drying in a rag, and empty eyes staring backwards at what is no longer there. In Berlin, of course, there are still the broken teeth of old buildings. As everybody knows, the Kaiser Wilhelm Church sticks out of the ground like a snapped bone. A grotesque totem. Meanwhile, the post-war architecture is as angelic as I am. Blank, imperial, modern, empty. Illegible, in the end. Nobody minds it. Berlin is an intensity of nothing, and I probably belong there. One gets pulled in so many directions, one can hardly move.

As a consequence of the area bombing that began in the late summer of 1940, the Nazis began building a series of mass bunkers in Berlin. In Kreuzberg, the Anhalter Hochbunker, completed in 1942, was originally meant for postal staff, railway workers, and passengers, but came to hold thousands upon thousands as conditions worsened. By 1945, the overcrowding was desperate. The Flakturm Tiergarten or 'Zoo Tower' (blown up by the British after the war) protected the government quarter. Defence against the Allied raids from the flak towers built in Berlin's parklands was on an industrial scale, with anti-aircraft ammunition being fed into hoppers before loading electronically into guns guided by radar. The Reichsbahnbunker Friedrichstrasse, a grand neoclassical edifice constructed under the general direction of Albert Speer, was built by captive Russians but used by the occupying Red Army as a gaol before the GDR turned it into a 'banana bunker', warehousing tropical fruit. The shelter in Schöneberg, meanwhile, is now being incorporated into—or rather, partially concealed by—a Brutalist social housing project that will squat over it for years to come. These bunkers were grey geometric mountains, immense concrete blisters, great slabs of endurance. Those that survive communicate a sense of permanence that is nonetheless cryptic, as if lacking memory. In the blink of an eye, they have become ancient, without speech. Old monsters turned to stone. Graffiti and posters and litter are all the energy that now emanates from them. Inert and alone, their persistence recalls only that compulsive type of self-protection from which there can be no possible benefit.

While Hitler built these preposterous caves for hordes of Berliners to suffocate in, in the United States Erich Mendelsohn—well-known expressionist architect, founding member of Der Ring, and pioneer of Streamline Moderne (known for its aerodynamic style, best exemplified by the corner design of the Mossehaus offices on Schützenstrasse)—collaborated with the U.S. Army and Standard Oil on the construction of 'German Village' in the Dugway Proving Ground in Utah. Having abandoned Germany in 1933, Mendelsohn was to be found a decade later helping the Americans create replicas of standard housing to assist plans for an aerial bombardment, specifically the firebombing that aimed to set Berlin ablaze. At Dugway they conducted early tests of chemical and biological weaponry, the main target being residential areas, the objective being the creation of an unstoppable firestorm in the heart of the city. The village itself recreated, with the utmost accuracy and attention to detail, the heavy furnishings of ordinary homes, the typical paint and woodwork, the clothes in the closet, the children's toys on the floor. It was a flammable Berlin that Mendelsohn helped simulate in Utah. At the start of the war, President Roosevelt had entreated all European combatants to confine bombings raids to military targets. France and Britain agreed, on condition their enemies did the same. But the British were noticeably quick to jettison that particular commitment, doing so explicitly and conspicuously after the Germans blitzed Rotterdam in May 1940. Berlin was bombed within weeks. Dortmund had been all but destroyed months before. An empty pledge to minimise the destruction of civilian property in military operations was not only rescinded—as Mendelsohn's village, burnt over and over again, amply testifies—it was completely reversed. At Dugway they also had a Japanese village. Comparative tests showed that, while it would catch more readily than Berlin, a German inferno (once lit) would probably be without end.

Firebombing relied on a concoction of high-explosives and incendiaries, first blowing out doors and windows, then burning buildings. Lightweight incendiaries set the attics alight, while more hefty firebombs decimated the lower floors. The flames merged at such speed that they soon formed firestorms rising a mile high, carrying the force of a hurricane. A thousand degrees of heat melted glass and asphalt and flesh. Charred, shrunken corpses lay twisted in burning pools of human fat. Some were boiled alive in bursting water. In the aftermath, escapees fought to board trains out of the city. Mothers who had gone mad carried baskets of toys and, occasionally, the cooked remains of a baby. Dead children were far from uncommon luggage among refugees, some of whom were so broken that they never once looked out of the train window. The survivors were little more than silent rubble. In the air raid shelters, flamethrowers were needed to burn off the thick crust of flies that blackened the black ruins. Bodies bloated with heat piled up in their flight from the roasting cellar walls. Dirt and hunger and ghosts were all that was left, and the occasional face that looked like a blood-pale fish gasping for breath. Snapped furniture and bones and air that was warped and dry.

In fact, long after the torching of Berlin, Freie Universität made its own bunker—the *Maüsebunker* or 'mouse bunker'—the spiralling costs of which delayed opening throughout the 1970s. The building is home to the Institute for Experimental Medicine, Free University's animal laboratory where thousands of rodents face scientific testing. The *Maüsebunker* is a Brutalist battleship, its blue ventilation turrets sticking out of concrete sloped walls like gunboat cannons, its flanks covered with little triangular windows that jut outwards like pyramidic barnacles. The whole edifice is topped with the recessed glass of a command bridge and great chimneys stretching upwards to the sky. The architect, Gerd Hänska, had been a student of Hans Poelzig's son. A sinister combination of Cold War machismo and biomilitary experimentation no doubt cements the futurism of Hänska's building. But underneath that, the sense of laboratory as bunker raises terrible ghosts of the past, recalling both the monumental dugouts and buried factories which fortified Speer's 'bridge of tradition' (before his Nazi years, Speer having been refused entry to the Poelzig studio for lack of imagination), and the prefabricated test sites of the exiled Mendelsohn. The storm of Total War comes in many forms, including the shelters where it is planned. Interminable defensive aggression. Speer was fortunate to survive Nuremberg. Having fallen from favour after the assassination attempt on Hitler in 1944, zealotry gave way to pragmatism. What saved him during the trial was that he rejected scorched earth and promoted himself as defender of the 'substance' of German industry. Speer awaited a post-war climate in which the protection of industrial captains could be relied upon. But a certain taste for eco-warfare could not be entirely repressed. Along with one of the directors of Siemens, he had conspired in a last-ditch plan to asphyxiate the Führer, Goebbels, and Boorman as they huddled in a chancellery bunker.

I didn't want to go up to Liesl's anymore, and it was senseless to hope she'd come to me all that much. We didn't talk about it, but I started to see her less from that time onwards. As the summer evenings passed, I tried to work more at night, to finish something for once. Sometimes we'd have a drink at a nearby bar we used after classes, a place where you could get a carafe of Italian wine, but I could tell her mind was elsewhere. Or at least I thought I could. I wonder now whether perhaps it was mine that had wandered. But all of a sudden it was as if she was behind plate glass, and I don't know if I put her there. I didn't think I could reach her. And our way of talking had changed. It was less alive somehow. She'd ask about my writing, but as I talked, I wasn't sure if either of us were listening. Our conversation was becoming telegraphic, as if a certain distance had scrambled the concision made possible by intimacy. I missed her, right there in front of me. She used to tease me about politics or literature or the clothes that I wore, but now she rarely came that close. And, more than ever, I wondered who she was. After a couple of drinks she'd mention that she had to be somewhere, and asked whether I'd come, and I'd give the excuses she expected.

It was an impasse neither of us had planned, even if the steps that led to it were not entirely unchoreographed. On one occasion we had been talking about a volume of Celan's poetry she wanted to borrow (a rare request, in fact), which left her without a reason to avoid coming up to my burrow of a place. As she sat and turned the pages, from across the room I noticed the strands of pale-yellow hair that had become loose near the nape of her neck. I walked over and tried to fix them, but I just made things worse. Without turning from her book, Liesl's fingers pulled at the tangle of straw and it spilled across her shoulders. I ran my hands through it, passing over her shoulders and back, my fingertips brushing her throat. Then she let go of the Celan and took hold of both my hands, pulling me closer to her, my face in her hair and against hers. With one hand she pushed my head against her lips, her hand over my mouth, until neither of us had any air. In the drowning stillness I felt a jolting urge to breathe and managed to gasp her name. Her nails pulled across my cheek, the palm of her hand pushing me away, and then she struck me, one hand after the other, her hair whipping across her face and mine, my lip split open, and suddenly her hands tightening around my wrists as I fell back on the bed. And she spat in my face and kissed my face hard and closing my eyes I felt the weight of her skull. I had called her Anna.

We didn't talk about that, either. After she'd gone, I picked up the book Liesl had left open—something she never did—and read the words on the page. Your hair is not brown. Your hand full of hours. The balance of grief, you are heavier than I. You smile at me from the depths. You whisper, 'they're filling the world with me now, it's time that you came here and kissed me'. Your hair is not brown.

NOTE VIII: Enclosed in a letter to Wilhelm Fliess, dated 24 January 1895, we find a draft of Freud's early ideas on paranoia, in which he includes a table that summarises the differences between hysteria, paranoia, hysterical psychosis, hallucinatory confusion, and obsession. These differences apply in a number of categories: affect (which is converted and dispensed with by the hysteric but retained by the paranoiac and obsessive alike); ideational content (in contrast to paranoid and psychotic subjects, hysterics and obsessives are not conscious of the idea that originally afflicts them, in the latter case because of substitution); and outcome. In terms of the latter, we are told, the psychotic fails in defending against their assailant, the hysteric manages an unstable defence but with satisfactory gain in psychic terms, whereas obsessive and paranoid types share a similar outcome: permanent defence without gain. Permanent defence without gain—what a situation to be in! A cold war condition, if ever there was one.

Almost exactly a year later, 1 January 1896, Freud writes once more to Fliess on the topic of the neuroses of defence (he playfully includes the subtitle: 'A Christmas Fairy Tale'), not only to distinguish between hysteria, obsession, and paranoia, but to further elaborate their connections. Each display different forms of pathological affect; each is responsible for a degree of damage that will doubtless become permanent. Defence involves, in general, the psychic repression of unpleasurable ideas or memories; exactly how this occurs, and the manner in which the repressed nevertheless returns, establishes specific differences between the various neuroses. Obsessional thinking, of course, involves conscious self-reproach, which is subsequently converted into a conscientiousness that overlays onto the affective condition of the sufferer an antithetical symptom: the compulsive behaviour itself. What is repressed returns in the form of a tormented scrupulousness that itself substitutes for the original trauma. Anxiety, shame, hypochondria, delusional fear of persecution—all give conscious shape and form to this substitution. The redoubling force of the compulsion—whether it entails brooding, a mania of doubt, hoarding, or bizarre ceremonial acts—is all that stands between these affects and an overwhelming crisis. Obsessional neurosis, writes Freud, can be cured if all the affective twists and turns of substitution are unravelled, leaving exposed only primary self-reproach, raw guilt, in the face of the original distress. But accomplishing this would involve working through an enormous number of intermediary ideas or compromise-formations, each of which in their turn provides the content of obsessional thinking. And Freud confesses to his conviction that it is impossible to entirely subdue repressed material through the efforts of conscious thought. On the contrary, repressed ideas prove themselves well capable of entering the most rational trains of thought. Which implies that the remedy may be poisoned, that the curative procedures of psychoanalysis might in fact encourage and indeed worsen neurotic illness. No plan survives contact with the enemy. The offensive itself hazards exposure to covert counter-forces. An extreme wariness is at risk of setting in, *folie du doute* dictates the terms of engagement. And, with that, Freud moves on in his letter to discuss paranoia. As cold as Christmas, where a day-long truce becomes frozen into a perpetual state, obsession is left in suspended animation.

THE MONUMENT TO THE UNKNOWN political prisoner was never built in Berlin. In the early 1950s the ICA ran an open competition for a sculpture to commemorate detainees caught up in political conflicts, not specifying any ideological or historical setting in particular. A young, international cast of entrants was targeted, and a thousand and a half designs were submitted, many of them abandoning figurative interpretation in favour of abstraction. Despite the apparent breadth and neutrality of the competition, artists from the Eastern Bloc refrained from entry amid Soviet suspicions that the CIA had been involved in financing the initiative. Sculptors of the calibre of Naum Gabo and Barbara Hepworth participated. The winner was Reg Butler, who had designed a stark metal framework resembling a watchtower or a radio mast standing on a great pedestal. Butler's final maquette was a tripod fashioned out of bronze wire, an asymmetrical Jacob's ladder made of poles of different lengths and heights crossed by horizontal bars and metal piping forming round-cornered rectangular shapes, like empty television sets. An earlier plan to include a single figure at the centre of the sculpture was abandoned, with three smaller ones – the 'watchers' – positioned at the base of the monument under two of its legs, looking up at a forgotten scaffold or cage. A conscientious objector, Butler had worked as a blacksmith during the war, and his work from the period was characterised by an expertise in forging and welding. Years later, he worried that the public would see the winning entry as merely a bob's worth of bent wire, a nice piece of abstract art, whereas a human element persisted in his imagination. The sculpture, he said, was a stage set high up, overlooking the world around.

Berlin's mayor had announced that his city would welcome the statue, although not without opposition from residents and with no guarantee of the necessary funding; his notion was to have the monument look eastwards from West Berlin over the Soviet zone. The idea of an apparently vacant turret from which unwitnessable panoramic domination might nevertheless be exercised is certainly a powerful theme for political thought in the post-war years. But it was never built, perhaps because it was too reminiscent of Berlin's wartime flak towers, perhaps because it seemed to call for a certain absence in terms that were nevertheless politically ambiguous.

Liesl had stopped coming to classes and she stopped picking up the phone. I let the days pass—maybe it was a few weeks—and I did nothing. And then I found myself travelling up to Kreuzberg now and again, walking the streets for a while, buying coffee where I'd been on the day I saw her in the blue dress, waiting around with no good reason to be there. Feeling a little sick at the people and the noise and the smell. In the end I found myself standing outside her building, although I think it took me a couple of trips to decide I would go in.

I climbed the stairs and knocked at the door. I waited, and knocked again, this time harder. I was about to knock for a third time when a neighbour appeared from the doorway across the hall. I asked him if he'd seen her.

—Miss Reissmann?

—Yes, Reissmann. I'm looking for her.

—Yes. But she has gone.

—When?

—Two weeks ago.

—Where?
—She didn't say. Except she was leaving West Berlin.
—Are you sure? I mean, did she leave anything behind?
—Nothing, no. Nothing at all. She left and then a man took everything from her place.
—Do you know who he was?
—I'm sorry. I can't tell you anything more. That's all I know.
—And she didn't leave a number?
—No.
—Am I the only one who has come looking?
—Please. I do not know.
He turned to go back inside. I called after him.
—Wait. Miss Reissmann. Did you know her well?
—Not well, no.
—Her first name?
—Liesl. It was Liesl. Now please, I'm sorry, I cannot help.

He shut the door and I stood in the hallway, realising I had hesitated to come because I already knew this would happen. I knew she was gone, and I knew her leaving would be absolute and irretrievable. I had nothing in my hands or in my pockets, and I thought suddenly that I'd lost my keys and my wallet, so I checked in my jacket and trousers and found them where they seemed not to have been. Downstairs, I checked the mail but there was nothing. Outside, the street was in bright sunlight, and it sounded of traffic and there was some shouting that was good-humoured although it did not seem so at first. I found I was crying, and I stood there for a moment and looked to the wall while people passed by. There was some grit in my pocket and some fibres of the lining had broken down and rolled together to form little pills that I turned between my fingers until the tears stopped. And then I went away, I went back to walk for an hour in the mottled light of the botanical gardens, strolling across checkerboard lawns beneath the American trees.

At the time I was in Berlin, the Neue Nationalgalerie bunker was showing *Richtkräfte einer neuen Gesellschaft* by Joseph Beuys. Liesl and I had seen it together. The work consisted of dozens upon dozens of blackboard panels marked with chalk which had been made during Beuys's lecture at the ICA in 1974, during a collaborative artistic initiative that was part of a 'German month' in London (funded because Britain had just joined the EEC). As he spoke about the relationships between art, politics, and society, Beuys wrote furiously on the boards, then fixed each one with spray before throwing them down on the floor with an explosive bang. That he wrote mostly in German before a largely English-speaking assembly heightened questions about the nature of the performance and its relationship to the political language and intentions of the event. For some, the immediate impact of Beuys's presence on stage seemed to jar with a rather abrasive sense of distance and controlled framing of space. The feeling of proximity stirred by an impassioned political address was complicated, for some, by the deliberate preservation of a technical aid—the supplementary notes on a blackboard—in the interests of the production of an artwork that would be presented under his sole name. How could the improvisational fluidity of the speaker be reconciled with the more contrived and calculated gesture of the artist? Beuys' relationship to audience and environment was always rather complex and involved: during a performance by John Cage at Kunstakademie Düsseldorf in 1964, he had locked the doors and refused the students exit, making a comparison with the nights he spent in bomb shelters as a child. Nevertheless, in his absence Beuys encouraged members of the public to walk over the boards scattered across the gallery as part of the *Richtkräfte einer neuen Gesellschaft* exhibit so they could carefully inspect the markings, every swirl of near-cryptographic writing mixing with bold diagrammatic strokes of chalk. Visitors could thereby participate in the physical aspects of artistic invention and language-creation performed in the original act of making, their footfall leaving its own embodied imprint as if to document a collective experience that persisted after the fact. That such an imprint might also be construed as damage brings up the idea that the repetition involved in the experience of the artwork is of a traumatic kind. And, of course, that experience is also a re-making, just as the artist's creative act itself entailed a certain repetitive trafficking between visual and verbal media, a constitutive exchange between linguistic and pictorial markings as much as a dialogue with those who were present. The Beuys piece encapsulated the paradox surrounding the detonation of every incendiary device. It was a controlled explosion that happened in the knowledge that its lasting effects would be incalculable. The blackboards were a bombsite.

Richtkräfte einer neuen Gesellschaft reminded me, at the time, of the first words of a text by the French-Algerian philosopher Jacques Derrida, 'La Double Séance', words which point in silence to quotations on a blackboard. 'La Double Séance' formed the occasion for two sessions presented in the Spring of 1969, half a decade before the Beuys (but at a mid-point between Düsseldorf and London), during which the members of Derrida's audience had been given a printed handout that included an excerpt from Plato's *Philebus* set alongside Stéphane Mallarmé's short prose work *Mimique*, the two forming vertical columns adjacent to one another—although, near the top of the page, Plato's Socrates overhung the poet to the tune of a dozen or so lines, making an inverted L-shape beneath which *Mimique* sheltered as if under the branches of a tree. The contrived topological typography of black letters on a white paper background was supplemented, across the room, by a series of other quotations written in white chalk on the blackboard, making a dense web of crossings and remarkings, the reader always going from one to the other, back and forth in a double and more-than-double movement. Black and white steps measured out across a chessboard seen in a looking glass. The conjunction of these two pieces of writing on a single sheet of paper provided a way to reprise the encounter between a Platonic idea of 'truth' and its supposed outside, Mallarmé's text allowing Derrida to restage the philosophical question of mimesis, imitation, or the copy. The idea of the mimetic has traditionally helped to organise philosophy's pejorative attitude to poetry, literature, and the arts. Imitation is typically framed in ontological terms, as the philosophers themselves might say—that is, by way of reference to an entity or a reality that is more original and replete, hence more truthful. The copy is always secondary and derivative. But by conjuring up a mime drama, the pantomime *Pierrot assassin de sa femme* by the French artiste Paul Margueritte, Mallarmé's *Mimique* itself mimes the philosophical discourse of mimesis found in the passage from Plato's *Philebus*; it fabricates a simulated version which resists reincorporation into the solemn construal of mimesis found in the Platonic doctrine. For the mime mimes nothing but the mimetic itself, without verity, without the solid grounding of reference, without the legitimating language of 'truth'. All it copies or repeats is the fragility of a distinction between the sober philosophical idiom and its own mimicry. The two are held apart by the most slender of veils; one scene of writing gets inscribed within the folds of the other. Derrida points to the exemplarity of a name that *Mimique* itself gives to such a slender veil — the hymen: 'The scene illustrates but the idea, not any actual action, in a hymen (out of which flows Dream), tainted with vice yet sacred, between desire and fulfilment, perpetration and remembrance: here anticipating, there recalling, in the future, in the past, *under the false appearance of a present*'. An enduring and uninterrupted fabric of allusion that breaks neither ice nor mirror, as the poet puts it. It is in the folds of this hymen that Plato and Mallarmé are to be found, as perhaps the stage-names of a perpetually entangled confrontation between philosophy and the arts, the original and the copy, the signified and the signifier, the referent and the sign, literature and truth. In the end, *Mimique* is that strange text which, by refusing thematic interpretation or ontological disclosure, resists the desire to unveil 'meaning'. Of course, I am thinking of Liesl. Of nothing else but her. Of her two names, and of the connection between them, which I now hesitate to describe as false.

Note ix: Obsession is, if not a rank stalemate, at the very least a permanent stand-off. In what James Strachey describes as one of the last strictly psychoanalytic writings published during Freud's lifetime, 'Analysis Terminable and Interminable' (1937), the founding father reflects on the various obstacles confronting a successful treatment. Here, Freud is thinking not only of the barriers which arise in particular circumstances as an individual analysis proceeds, but of the more persistent obstacles faced by psychoanalysis now that it has reached a certain level of maturity as an established practice over several decades. His essay therefore proceeds on the basis of a sustained analogy between the lasting impact of psychoanalytic treatment on individual patients and the question of psychoanalysis's durability itself.

Freud begins by observing that psychoanalytic therapy, if conducted rigorously, is 'a time-consuming business'. If analysis itself had developed on the strength of its initial resistance to the impatience of medical science with the extended treatment of mental illness, nevertheless as time went by certain practitioners sought to innovate with psychoanalytic methods in order to shorten its duration. Otto Rank's attempt to pinpoint primal trauma as the key to expediting psychic recovery is singled out for note by Freud. Presumably the benefits of a more truncated approach would not be lost on prospective patients or their families; more widely, the optimism displayed by Rank concerning his own supposed breakthrough fitted perfectly with the climate of hope and prosperity found in 1920s America, presented by Freud as in stark contrast to the seemingly never-ending misery of post-war Europe. Rank's procedure was therefore a child of its time, designed to adapt the tempo of analytic therapy to the pace of American life. For Freud, however, Rank's brainchild was both foolishly premature and destined to be short-lived. It is likened to the comic scenario of a fire-brigade tackling a blazing house-fire by removing the overturned oil-lamp that caused it. No doubt a considerable shortening of the brigade's activities would be effected by this means, the author quips drily. In the end, time is the only thing that is saved.

Freud nevertheless takes this anecdote as a cue to reflect on his own efforts to speed up analytic treatment. Just before hostilities broke out in 1914, Freud had chosen to address the disappointing results of treatment in the case of one of his patients by fixing an impending deadline for its termination. The patient in question—that wealthy Russian whose progress was impeded by a level of complacency brought on by the partial success of early analysis—was forced to confront his deeper problems with greater haste by means of withdrawing the reassurance of unlimited treatment. At the time, the results were misleadingly promising. When he left me in the midsummer of 1914, says Freud, with no more inkling than the rest of us about what lay just around the corner, I thought his cure was complete. But, like an all-consuming house-fire, the unforeseen effects of a devastating world war and, on top of that, an aristocratic fall from grace quickly reversed the short-term gains of an abruptly concluded analysis.

Freud goes on to evaluate the risks of an early termination of therapy. An artificially imposed conclusion might potentially work, but only if the timing is right. And one doesn't get second chances—Freud recalls the saying that a lion only springs once, which he insists must apply in such cases. The prospect of a manufactured ending must constitute neither an empty threat nor a false promise. But the trouble is that one can never know when the time is right. And not just because it is difficult to establish whether progress is sufficient to conclude treatment. In any analysis, aspects of the patient's childhood history may be slow in coming to light. Indeed, they might powerfully resist analysis. They may remain hidden or become distorted as a consequence of therapy itself. Apparent improvements may well conceal the actual preservation of more entrenched obstacles to analytic success. Termination on the strength of an assessment of progress is therefore as likely to be ill-considered as it may be expertly judged.

Freud moves on from the question of analysis's duration to the problem of its possible end. He does so, in a double sense. The issue is not only when treatment should stop; the real difficulty is, what is analysis actually *for*? From the second part of the essay onwards, Freud considers the relentless struggle between, on the one hand, constitutional factors causing traumatic conditions for the analysand, and, on the other, the power of the ego strengthened by psychoanalysis to defend itself against their continual onslaught. Here, even if analysis initially produces positive results, illness can always recur—prompting the question of whether a relapse is due to incomplete treatment of the original ailment, or whether it may spring from a wholly new expression of psychic conflict that could not have been foreseen or forestalled. Freud takes a moment to imagine the lively debate between the sceptic who draws from this state of affairs the gloomy conclusion that, regardless of its provisional achievements, psychoanalysis is ultimately bound to falter, and the more ambitious optimist who believes that psychoanalytic practice has not yet developed to its mature end. Advances in analytic technique once more echo the situation of the individual for whom the duration of analysis is a key question: while in retrospect a degree of scepticism seems justified concerning the resolution of a case, equally it is always too soon to tell whether something better can be expected in future. In other words, the idea that one shouldn't be too quick to pronounce endings is as much as source of hope as it is a reason for despair.

In light of such ambivalent circumstances, the capacity of psychoanalysis to protect its patients against subsequent relapse remains a question that Freud is reluctant to dismiss. Even if one cannot permanently remove some constitutional defects, would it be possible through the workings of the initial analysis to insure against certain types of recurrence? But here is the problem: since psychoanalysis seeks to positively adjust the ego by reinforcing its defences, the instinctual forces it aims to combat will themselves undoubtedly toughen up. It therefore provokes an enduring show of strength, or in fact an arms race. Analysis as deterrence therefore provokes deepening anxiety; a managed peace begins to look like brinkmanship. Freud wonders if, in order to stop future conflicts from wheeling out of control, present ones might be deliberately stirred up. A pre-emptive strike, in other words, or indeed preventive war. He seems to dismiss the thought. The protective procedure, he says, must not risk the same degree of danger that the illness itself threatens. But, still, the deliberate arousing of conflict in the patient's imagination may be tactically justified. War, however one might name it, is a time-consuming business whose scheming nevertheless works on intensely narrow margins.

NOW THAT I LOOK BACK at that time in Berlin, I remember several things. I remember the clouds and, after the rain, how clear the sky would sometimes be. I remember the traffic and the parks, like sea and land, and the places where it was noisy and dirty and dark before the hour. A type of energy somewhere between living and dying caught the wind as it rattled through the streets. I read, alone in my room, more than I had done anywhere else. I recall reading, late one night, that Robert Walser's texts had been described as acts of 'inner emigration', which makes them angelic, now I think about it. I remember my students less well, which is an indictment in itself. I couldn't tell you exactly what I was writing, about Dürrenmatt or anything else. I can guess why I can't. I remember Liesl. I don't know if these memories mean anything. I'm conscious they come to life because they're from a future I haven't yet reckoned with, that I couldn't possibly know. Memory is a burning archive whose cinders scald the air one breathes. It is nothing but the disquiet to be suffered tomorrow. I don't know I have the energy for it. I want to go back to sleep, and I don't want to sleep. She was somebody I shouldn't have loved, because it ricochetted like a lost bullet, but I love her and I wish I could forget. I'd like not to think about anything except books. I'm scared of boredom and loneliness but it's hard to stand anything or anyone. Nobody sees me, and that's a relief. Why can't I forget? I wonder if she's a false memory that stops me facing something real. I remember her hands pulling mine, her hands on my head and over my mouth. You breathe in, underwater, and it's a relief. You can rest. And then panic and then nothing. Her hair was like caramel.

I'm going to put out the light. I can't read.

I remember Liesl telling me something her mother, Krystyna, used to say when she was a child. She said that there were three rooms, when you die, and you had to make a choice. In the first room, you would be confronted with everything that you regretted or had caused you pain, the entire sum of your unhappiness, and you would be asked to consider each of your many sorrows in turn, until you reconciled yourself to all of them. Presumably you'd find some peace when the last of it was done. But since a lifetime of anguish can be caused by a momentary event or by a decision made in a single instant—most decisions having been taken either far too soon or too late—nobody could tell how long you might spend in such a room. In the second, you would be able to enjoy everything that made you happy, every warm memory, each person that you had loved or had loved you, everything that tasted good or felt or sounded good or had given you pleasure. You would be able to turn over in your hands each small satisfaction and every memorable achievement. But as you considered them each would slip away, not unhappily but in the way a good meal is digested, until everything was gone. In the last room, you would simply begin again, but with nothing—without wisdom or memory or any vestige of yourself. You would be wiped from a clean slate. Liesl said that when her mother told this story she would always make the same choice and ask whether it was the right one. 'I wonder,' her mother would say. And that would be that. I remember Liesl laughed as she told me about it, saying it was just a piece of folkish mysticism from Eastern Europe. 'But I thought you were from Wittenberg?' I said. 'My mother was originally from Kottbus,' she said (which is near the Polish borders). 'But what choice do you think I made?' I guessed that it was always the last one, and she smiled. 'I know which you'd choose,' she said. And perhaps she did. But I can't think why I didn't ask about Kottbus.

That she was an informant is as likely as anything else. I can see her reasons. For myself, what reason did I have? To call her by another name, I mean, knowing what the consequences might be. I doubt she was from Wittenberg at all. Perhaps, like me, she was even an orphan of sorts. When she kissed me and spat at me it was the same thing. Anyway, nothing happened except she was gone. Memory is a form of thinking, that's all. We would never find ourselves in the same room again, Liesl and I, not in this life or the next. Towards the end of a novel from his Berlin years, *Geschwister Tanner*, Walser recounts an imagined fairy tale: Once there were snowflakes that, having nothing better to do, fell to earth, some into the fields or onto rooftops, or they began to lay on the hats and caps of people in the town or, in one instance, on the eyelashes of a horse hitched to a cart. One found its way indoors, through an open window, and no word of it was heard afterwards. In the alleys and in the forest, the snow fell. There was a man blackened with filth who longed to wash. Lacking soap and warm water, he went out into the street to bathe in the falling snow. His face was clean again, but he developed a bad cough and for some reason he had to wait until winter returned the following year, then he ran into the mountains and met a child, a beggar, with a snowflake in its hand like a delicate flower. The child offered the snowflake to the man, and he ate it and was cured of his cough. Now the skies were dark and the child sat alone among the trees, having been beaten earlier that day without knowing the reason why. The child knew very little, and despite the conditions its bare feet were not cold. Perhaps it froze to death during the night, but it was in any case too small to feel a thing. God saw the child but was too big to do anything about it. I thought that, as the falling snow clung to the earth, what stuck to it and made it dissolve or harden into ice was the intelligence of an evil that would never be acted upon. Simon, the hero of Walser's book, wards off a freezing winter by washing in cold water until his flesh glows, and by walking back and forth across the room on his hands. By wrapping his feet in a coat while he sits at his desk, rather than wearing it outside. A biting wind drives him into the forest and up towards the mountains, along a track that leads him to the place where a wooden chalet once stood in which his brother used to paint, now converted into a health resort. Inside it is warm and bustling with people. Taking a seat at a little table, Simon is ignored for a considerable while. The proprietor, noticing he is unattended, makes a special case of him. She chatters away until he all but succumbs to the tedium of her hospitality. With graceless simplicity she talks and talks about the goodness of dreaming and hopes for the future; even though he has said nothing, she confesses him to be an infuriating distraction, the very embodiment of wasted time. All the while talking, almost for as long as anyone could bear it. The hall begins to empty when at last Simon is asked about himself. Not because he is especially interesting, but perhaps from pity, perhaps worry, perhaps plain intrigue at the prospect of an unheard voice. Our hero responds with a long précis of the novel in which he has just featured, telling of his brother Kaspar, the painter, now living in Paris, his hair unkempt. The laziness of his school years, the effort of painting not dissimilar to that of a fallen horse heaving itself from the ground. Then the oldest brother Klaus—a prominent scholar, thoughtful, considerate, the picture of forbearance. Emil, the last of four boys, a remote figure institutionalised in an asylum. Hedwig, the young schoolmistress sequestered in a little village, who after three months evicts her freeloading brother with a contemptuous kiss, leaving goodbyes unswallowed in his mouth. Three months of conversation that rustled like a mother's skirts. After which, our hero embarks on a succession of short-lived employments that recall the opening pages of the book. By this time Simon has entirely outtalked his hostess, now apparently the hostage of his charms. All that remains is for her to tempt him into the snow-swept woods with the promise of a good schooling in the art of whispers. I think that, in Krystyna's parable, a fourth door should open onto this forest lodge. Especially given the autobiographical character of *Geschwister Tanner*. But now it's too late to tell Liesl, even if it makes her wrong about me, about the choice I'd make. We'll never find ourselves in the same room again, not in this life or any other. Liesl was pale and tall, with blonde eyelashes and freckled skin, and her hair looked like damp straw. There were always Filter Kings in her bag, but she never smoked them, and unopened letters, I.D., tissues and receipts, broken pens and old keys, blank postcards and nameless photos, and the make-up she almost never wore. Her skirt was always shorter than her coat, and for some reason nobody lost patience that she was never on time.

NOTE X: To summarise these notes, to date. The obsessive is embattled and alone, plagued by the madness of doubt as much as by an epistemophilic mania that feeds upon false connections, and chasing connections that may be falsely false. Incapable of making contact without indulging in the hygiene of self-recrimination. Sick with worry. Stricken at any moment by the infantile affect which clings to buried trauma. Hoarding, brooding over, ritualising their loneliness. Embroiled in a phony war without end but also without beginning. Permanent defence without gain. Living on the borderlines of a frozen conflict, they store memories like broken toys or watches that have stopped, holding and hating and exhausting them as well as themselves. They are the living dead. Pitiless, blank, abandoned buildings blackened by the flames. They cannot go on, but they do, the restless souls that cannot be weighed. Despite every compromise, every substitution, they are the same at the end as at the beginning. The traces they leave are night-time cryptograms, ciphers of a dream. One would never know them, not even when they are gone. If one listened carefully enough, all that might be heard is the urge to breathe.

A BALLOON CAN MAKE A NUISANCE of itself. In 1938, the British Balloon Command was established to protect key targets such as ports, harbours, cities, and industry – the plan being that barrage balloons, to which upward steel cables and explosives were attached, would force dive-bombers to climb to a higher altitude where anti-aircraft fire could be more effective. However, after concerns that wayward dirigibles might harm domestic power lines (worries that were borne out when, on a stormy night in September 1940, British balloons got loose, causing damage to railways, radio and power lines across the North Sea in Sweden and Denmark), a study was commissioned which suggested some military advantage may be gained through an outward campaign. While the defensive use of kite balloons became less effective as the war went on (the Germans switching from dive-bombing to high-level area bombardment, and then equipping V-1 bombs with wire-cutters on their wings), deployment over enemy lines was felt to be worthwhile. The inflatables trailed steel wires that could short-circuit high voltage power cables. They carried explosive devices to start fires in the fields and forests of Germany, the latter tactic aimed largely at inconveniencing the enemy, diverting human resources from the war effort by generating the need for constant fire-watching. These radio-controlled balloons were rough devices, capable of travelling only short distances and featuring the most basic mechanisms to regulate altitude; but they were cheap to produce – just a few shillings apiece – meaning that their economic impact was calculated to be far in excess of cost. In fact, an Admiralty surplus of over one hundred thousand weather balloons bumped up the supply. Winds above sixteen-thousand feet—the height of this airborne pestilence—mainly blew from west to east across the border, limiting the possibility of German retaliation. A thin wire (much thinner than those designed to thwart dive-bombers) dragged from a barrage balloon could cause a circuit-breaking arc of sufficient heat to melt the aluminium casing of steel conductors, exposing them to damage from the elements even if they were not fully severed. The dirigibles carried a range of incendiary gadgets with memorable names like beer, jelly, and socks (the first containing the explosive in half-pint bottles, the second featuring combustible cubes of gel in a can, the last holding its paraffin-soaked material in long thin canvas bags that, when released, bent like German sausages and hooked themselves onto trees). After the campaign began in earnest in Spring 1942, forest fires were reported in East Prussia and near Berlin. Until their effective retirement in 1944, when the intensity of the Allied air campaign made them more perilous than useful to the British bombers, these balloons were an embarrassment to the German forces. The Luftwaffe, it is said, had to be mobilised to shoot them down.

During the 1950s, meanwhile, more than half a million hydrogen inflatables were released from West Germany along the Czechoslovakian border, carrying food parcels and propaganda leaflets to the citizens of Eastern Europe. The balloons themselves were not officially state-sanctioned but were instead largely the products of U.S.-funded anti-communist organisations like Radio Liberty. The West Berlin authorities worried about the friction they caused with the East Germans. As the practice continued into the 1960s, one such device was described by the State Department as akin to a 'child's toy equipped with a primitive fuse that burned until contact was made with the skin of the balloon, causing it to explode'. A toy turned into a bomb that burns the skin is perhaps a more apt description of these supposedly benign propagandist tools. Meanwhile, wayward meteorological balloons which caught the eastward wind troubled the traffic corridors that linked Western Europe to West Berlin but also provoked Soviet suspicions, with fighter aircraft taking to the skies on more than one occasion.

In the early 1940s, Carl Jung wrote about the archetypal motif of the child. It is as if this archetype poses a conundrum, the solution to which is perhaps a balloon. Whether a rescuer, a little god, or an evil omen, the Jungian child floats up from a mythical dream. Sometimes a crown prince, sometimes the progeny of witches. Sometimes leaping out of a flower-cup or a golden egg, like a rare and distant treasure. Sometimes formed from the pieces of chtonic animals, snakes, or monkeys. Sometimes returning, like the dead, from an epic crossing. Such children open the doorway to a past that haunts us, irreconcilably, like a dream we should never have had; like the dream of flying which, for Jung, led in the end to carpet bombing. Yet the child-archetype promises redemption of the very same conflict for which they stand. Because of this double meaning, the motif of the child is often conveyed by roundness, by something circular, something curving back on itself. Jung concedes that a darker sense of infancy may well be coupled with a discordant, schizophrenic multiplicity (he speaks of swarming homunculi and roaming gangs of dwarfs), but the child can also become connective tissue, an elastic membrane stretched out over a void, pulling tight across thin air. Because a child is the miraculous solution to an unresolvable predicament, its archetype emerges, in Jung's own terms, as 'entelechy': absolute natality, pure potential. It is as though the child floats up all by itself, and its precariousness is as legendary as its heroism. 'Smaller than small and bigger than big': inflated, rarefied grandeur and desperate fragility, all at once, each beyond measure. The child-archetype is capable of astonishing flights and dizzying perils: a pinprick, or the laughter of a little bird. A vessel one can neither empty nor fill, as Jung puts it: a balloon is perhaps the answer to the riddle of the child. Like a child, it can make a nuisance of itself. But it can be a dangerous toy.

During his Berlin years Robert Walser took a balloon ride out to the Baltic coast, and afterwards wrote a story. But I won't say much more about that, except that his prose is more afloat, more dream-like, lighter and more unbreathable than anything else I know of. An air balloon is a double thing, compelled by forces that push and pull it upwards and downwards at the same time, pulling and pushing from the inside and the outside, expanding warming cooling contracting conspicuous invisible above away found lost. No more than a fine skin held taught by an invisible pressure of gases which hardens where the air begins to thin. And always on the verge of flames.

But a balloon is an ingenious way to cross a border, nonetheless—if the wind direction is in your favour. If not, you must reckon with the risks of being blown backwards, sucked backwards, with the chance of becoming lost in a vacuum, of falling, suffering a kind of weightlessness that, upon impact, explodes into its exact opposite. Of crossing back over a crossed border, like the *Volkesdeutsche* targeted by the BdV after the war. Expulsions from the east were not as chaotic and unplanned as they may have seemed. Satellite states looked to the Soviet Union to guarantee the benefits of a population transfer of so-called ethnic Germans, to secure the economic rewards of their repatriation westwards; but Stalin also nurtured a desire for protection among his newfound children in the east, particularly at the borders.

On the banks of the Oder, on both shores—in towns like Kottbus, for instance—it was this politics of a double-crossing migration that blew in the wind. In East Prussia, the Germans that remained in Soviet territory were conscripted as forced labour, having been forbidden to leave. But the flight of many, nonetheless, left behind a generation of *Wolfskinder*, wolf children living in the forests, some of them used by Lithuanian farmers, some put on trains to Soviet-occupied Germany, many arriving after a week-long journey without knowing who they were, each of them surviving by any means possible, if they survived at all. Many arriving dead, having suffocated or starved. Those that lived and were adopted by the East Germans doubtless enjoyed the roulette wheel of all wartime urchins.

Jung's child-archetype is born of irresolvable conflicts in the unconscious, of an unknowable strife that is forever lost. Its background is not just uncertain, but inexplicable. And yet by some inhuman wonder it emerges. A double miracle: one might be tempted to call it the impossible fate of an orphan birth. As likely as breathing underwater or floating on thin air. I sometimes want Liesl here, with me, so I'd know where I was, even if that place was nowhere—but, I tell myself, that would be a misreckoning. I tell myself that.

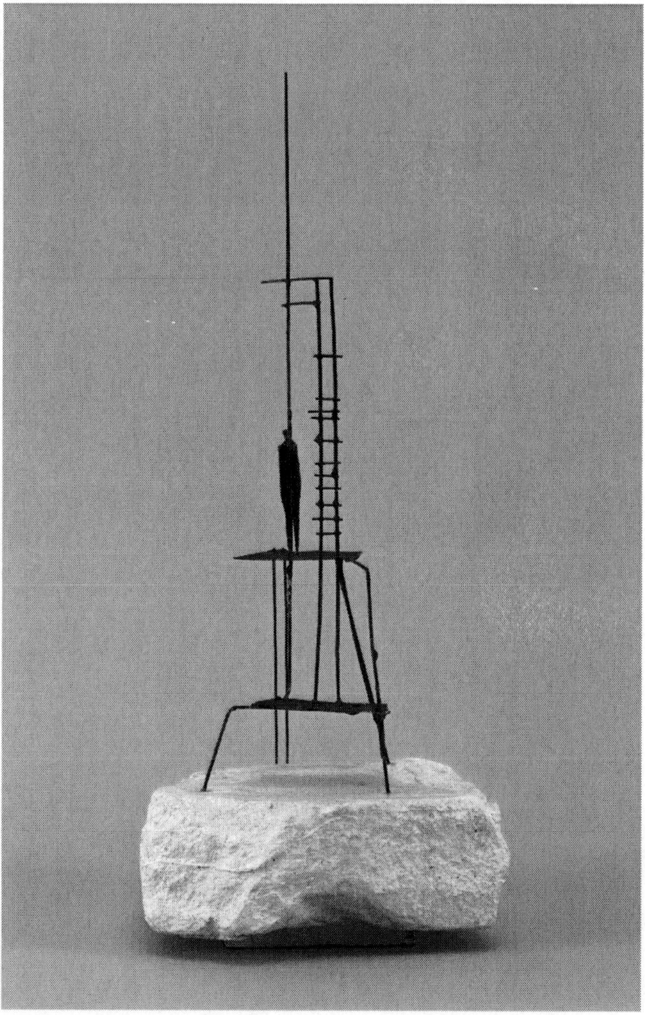